HERE'S HOW TO REACH ME

HERE'S HOW TO REACH ME

Matching Instruction
to Personality Types
in Your Classroom

by

Judith A. Pauley, Ph.D.

Dianne F. Bradley, Ph.D.

and

Joseph F. Pauley

Process Communications, Inc.

·P·A·U·L·H·
BROOKES
PUBLISHING Cᵒ ®

Baltimore • London • Sydney

Paul H. Brookes Publishing Co.
Post Office Box 10624
Baltimore, Maryland 21285-0624

www.brookespublishing.com

Typeset by A.W. Bennett, Inc.,
Hartland, Vermont.
Manufactured in the United States of America by
Versa Press, East Peoria, Illinois.

Illustrations of personality types are provided
courtesy of Clinton Powell.

Individuals described herein are composites, pseudonyms,
or fictional accounts based on actual experiences. Individuals'
names have been changed and identifying details have been
altered to protect their confidentiality.

Second printing, September 2003.

Library of Congress Cataloging-in-Publication Data

Pauley, Judith A.
  Here's how to reach me : matching instruction to personality types in
your classroom / by Judith A. Pauley, Dianne F. Bradley, Joseph F. Pauley.
      p.   cm.
  Includes bibliographical references and index.
  ISBN 1-55766-566-4
  1. Learning, psychology of.   2. Cognitive styles in children.
3. Typology (Psychology)   4. Teaching. I. Bradley, Dianne F., 1944–
II. Pauley, Joseph F. III. Title.

LB1060 .P38   2002
      370.15'23—dc21   2001043950

British Library Cataloguing in Publication data
are available from the British Library.

CONTENTS

About the Authors vii

Foreword *Taibi Kahler, Ph.D.* xi

Foreword *Jacqueline S. Thousand, Ph.D.* xiii

Acknowledgments xix

Introduction xxiii

Chapter 1 What Is Process Communication? 1

Chapter 2 Rosie Reactor (The Feeler) 33

Chapter 3 Will Workaholic (The Thinker) 43

Chapter 4 Paul Persister (The Believer) 53

Chapter 5 Doris Dreamer (The Imaginer) 63

Chapter 6 Rita Rebel (The Funster) 75

Chapter 7 Peter Promoter (The Doer) 87

Chapter 8 An Ounce of Prevention: How Process
Communication Integrates with Other
Learning Theories 101

Chapter 9 Keeping Students Out of Distress 115

Chapter 10 A Pound of Cure: Engaging All Students
in the Learning Process 141

Chapter 11 Keeping Teachers Out of Distress 169

References 197

Appendix 201

Index 209

ABOUT THE AUTHORS

Judith A. Pauley, Ph.D., Chief Executive Officer, Process Communications, Inc., 6701 Democracy Boulevard, Suite 300, Bethesda, MD 20817

Dr. Judith A. Pauley retired in 1999 from a distinguished, 42-year career teaching chemistry and physics in high school, college, and graduate school in the United States of America and Asia. She received numerous awards for her teaching methods and was named science teacher of the year by the Maryland Association of Science Teachers, Trinity College, and the Society of Sigma Xi. She is one of the founders of the Maryland Chemathon, is a past president of the Montgomery County Maryland Science Fair Association and the Chemical Educators of Maryland, and serves on the boards of several scientific organizations, including the Maryland Association of Science Teachers. She has presented extensively at local, national, and international science, science teaching, at-risk, dropout prevention, and other teaching conferences. She has written several articles on science teaching and helping every student succeed in the classroom and contributed to *Restructuring for Caring and Effective Education: Piecing the Puzzle Together, Second Edition* (Villa & Thousand, Brookes Publishing Co., 2000).

Dr. Pauley is Chief Executive Officer of Process Communications, Inc., which provides training on the Process Communication Model (PCM) and the discoveries of Dr. Taibi Kahler. She is the mother of three children, including a daughter with Down syndrome for whom she has been a lifelong advocate.

Dianne F. Bradley, Ph.D., Vice President, Process Communications, Inc., 6701 Democracy Boulevard, Suite 300, Bethesda, MD 20817

Dr. Dianne F. Bradley is a retired teacher and educational administrator. She has taught in both general education and special education classrooms from elementary school to graduate school and is an authority on successfully including students with disabilities in general education classrooms. She has written many articles on inclusive education and on helping every student succeed and is a co-author of *Teaching Students in Inclusive Settings* (Allyn & Bacon, 1997). She has presented extensively at local, national, and international education conferences on inclusive education and on helping every child succeed in the classroom, including the Association for Supervision and Curriculum Development (ASCD) and Council for Exceptional Children (CEC). Dr. Bradley has considerable experience supervising and mentoring new teachers and has done many in-service presentations for educators in applying the concepts of Process Communication in the classroom to reach and teach every child. She is an Adjunct Professor of Education at Johns Hopkins University in Maryland and Trinity College in Washington, D.C., and is the Vice President for Education of Process Communications, Inc.

Joseph F. Pauley, President, Process Communications, Inc., and Vice President for Education, Kahler Communications, Inc., 1301 Scott Street, Little Rock, Arkansas 72202

Joseph F. Pauley has taught at all levels, from elementary school through graduate school. He lived in Asia for 21 years and is an authority on cross-cultural communication and motivating people from other cultures. He has trained teachers in the internationally acclaimed concepts of PCM for the past 15 years to help them reach every student. He has presented extensively at local, national, and international conferences, including the National Dropout Prevention and At-Risk Student conferences sponsored by Clemson University. He has presented at the American Association for the Advancement of Science (AAAS), ASCD, National Science Teachers' Association (NSTA), and CEC conferences and at summer institutes sponsored by the University of Vermont and California State University, San Marcos. He has written several articles on ways to reach every student and contributed to *Restructuring for Caring and Effective Education: Piecing the Puzzle Together, Second Edition* (Villa & Thousand, Brookes Publishing Co., 2000), and to *Making It Happen: Student Involvement in Education Planning, Decision Making, and Instruction* (Wehmeyer & Sands, Brookes Publishing Co., 1998).

Mr. Pauley is the President of Process Communications, Inc., and Vice President for Education at Kahler Communications, Inc., which provides communication skills training to schools, businesses, and government agencies. He is the father of three children, including a daughter with Down syndrome for whom he has been a lifelong advocate.

FOREWORD

Parents and teachers are the most significant influences shaping and guiding the lives of our children. It is only fitting that three people who are teachers and parents, as well as experts in the Process Communication Model (PCM), wrote this book.

PCM has been applied in the fields of business, management, team building, sales, parenting, mentoring, religion, health, and education for more than two decades. Growing out of my Process Therapy clinical model, PCM has touched the lives of more than a million people on four continents, including presidents, generals, senators, astronauts, chief executive officers, professors, superintendents, principals, teachers, parents, and students. One former president of the United States publicly declared to a Secretary of Education that this model of learning and teaching is a "work of genius" and "a great contribution to education."

As teachers, parents, and educators, our mission is to significantly enhance the quality of people's lives (including our own) for generations. For us to succeed in this endeavor, we must help children learn in ways that best suit or fit each of them. The application of PCM to teaching and educating does just that by showing teachers which communication style will work best to connect with each student, how to motivate each student individually, and how to resolve conflicts and behavior problems by understanding each student's needs. Backed by a solid foundation of research (including several dissertations), PCM promises to be one of the most significant contributions to the field of education.

This book takes you into the real world of the educational process. You get to experience six different personality types from the perspective of both students and teachers—how they feel, how they think, and how they act. You will know why kids do what they do, and how you as an educator or parent can connect with them and help motivate them the *way they need to be motivated* in order to learn, grow, and prosper *in the ways that are naturally best for them.*

Intervention and prevention strategies are provided to reach each and every student. Also, other learner-centered approaches are integrated into the application of PCM in the educational setting. The great news about this model is that it works without the teacher having to learn additional content. The simple key is to use what each of us already possesses—some or all of these personality types in varying degrees. As we learn about and develop the various parts of ourselves, we can interact (process) with each student's personality type from that very same part of ourselves.

I am lucky to have discovered the fabric that holds together our process of communication. I am fortunate to live in a time when educators care deeply about their children and are devoted to helping them learn. And finally, I am blessed to have as friends Dr. Judy Pauley and Joe Pauley, who have devoted their lives to education, as has our colleague and co-author, Dr. Dianne Bradley. Thank you, Judy, Joe, and Dianne. Thousands of people will read your words. Your impact will be felt for generations.

Taibi Kahler, Ph.D.
Founder and Developer of the Process Communication Model
President, Kahler Communications, Inc.
Little Rock, Arkansas

FOREWORD

I first became familiar with the Process Communication Model (PCM) in the early 1990s when I met Joe and Judy Pauley, two of the three co-authors of this book, and their daughter Cecelia. We had come to know one another after they had been referred to me through a colleague who knew that I had been working on issues of disability rights in schools through a federal model demonstration grant. At the time, they were living in Maryland and I was working and living in Vermont, a state that has a reputation for being one of the most progressive with regard to including children and youth with disabilities in general education.

After a few phone conversations, Cecelia, Judy, Joe, and I finally met. Over the course of the next months and years we worked together closely, along with others such as Richard Villa and Dianne Bradley, to ensure that Cecelia would be fully included in her high school general education classes and extracurricular experiences. As a result of our collaboration Cecelia was able to participate fully in such activities as the varsity football cheerleading squad, choir, and Spanish club. Cecelia graduated along with her classmates in 1996 and went on to have community, college, and work experiences, which she continues to enjoy and to which she continues to make wonderful contributions. She even wrote a chapter on her successes for an important book on inclusive practices in schools (Pauley, Pauley, & Pauley, 2000). By the way, Cecelia happens to have Down syndrome and also happens to have the same personality base as I do. We have as our foundational personality type what you will come to know as the Rebel, so we connect easily and playfully, just as fun-loving Rebels happen to do!

Early on in our years of growing friendship, I was introduced to the concepts and processes of PCM. I received training from Joe and Judy on the emerging application of PCM to students at risk of school failure. I immediately saw the potential for PCM to transform not only teacher–student relationships within public school classrooms, but educator–educator, administrator–educator, administrator–community, and professor–university student relationships in elementary, secondary, and higher education contexts. During my last several years at the University of Vermont in the 1990s, the Pauley family graciously agreed to make frequent trips to Vermont to teach professors in the College of Education and my students in an advanced post-master's special education graduate program. With their guidance, we learned the latest version of the creative transformation of PCM into a working model that educators could use to eliminate miscommunication and conflict and maximize success with students.

Since 1996, I have lived and taught in California, preparing special educators who are new to the field as well as master's-level, experienced special educators. It has been a goal to bring to my campus the same instruction regarding PCM that so transformed my post-master's students in Vermont. The completion of this book, *Here's How to Reach Me: Matching Instruction to Personality Types in Your Classroom*, is a much-awaited tool that I will use to provide PCM studies as an option in our College of Education's advanced leadership coursework and in field experiences in special education. I am thrilled that the special educators I teach now have ready access to the PCM tools through the well-articulated content of this book.

All teachers can greatly benefit from applying PCM in their classrooms. Special educators, especially, need this knowledge and these skills because they are the ones who students turn to most when they experience misunderstanding and distress. These students express their distress through "rule-violating" behaviors and words and require someone to quickly craft interventions and supports to get things back on track. The procedures, forms, and valuable insights on ways of perceiving and communicating offered in this book are critical intervention tools that special educators and others can use to assist students in distress.

Why am I such a strong advocate of PCM for educators, youth who are perceived as troubled or troubling, or, for that matter, any person who is on a journey to psychological well being? It is because I have seen it work wonders in diverse arenas. I have used it to defuse potential crises in my personal and professional life. I have observed others use it with similar success. My former students and colleagues who received PCM training with Joe and Judy in Vermont continue to e-mail, phone, and send notes about critical situations with students, loved ones, and colleagues that have been resolved by remembering and applying what they had learned.

I am a much better teacher of adults as a consequence of PCM. I no longer judge students as wrong or contrary for the way in which they express their distress and the way they experience and react to the world when they "go to their personal basements." (You will find out what that means as you read further through the chapters.) Instead, I try to use the personality-based verbal and body language they need in order to get them to "hear" me, to know that I am listening and understanding, and that I am willing to work with them to reestablish equilibrium. I know to listen for and use verbs that "speak" to each student's base or current phase personality type. For example, I know that individuals who have Persister as a primary personality type use and respond to verbs that express their strong values base—verbs such as "believe." I also know that those who have Workaholic as a primary type are thinkers and respond to "thinking" and "knowing" verbs. In contrast, verbs such as these put off people who have Reactor as a primary personality type; you see, they need "feeling" verbs in their conversations. I also have learned through PCM that asking a question versus telling someone what I want or need works for most personality types, but not the Promoter and Dreamer types. They like and/or need direct communication.

At this moment, I suspect you may be "believing," "thinking," or "feeling" that what you are about to read in this book is going to be an overwhelmingly complex and impossibly dense amount of information to digest, incorporate into your personal and professional communication approaches, and systematically apply. I grant you that this book does offer a tremendous amount of information, but I promise you that it all will make great sense once you get into it. The authors carefully bring the information to life for you through examples, stories, and clear and simple planning and intervention tools. Their intent is that you will feel ready to go out and apply what you are learning and that you will experience immediate and sometimes remarkable results. As with most things in life, you will get better with conscious practice and reflection. You will change others' ways of communicating through your modeling. You will get others interested in learning about and knowing what you know about PCM so that they can communicate with children, youth, and adults as effectively as you do.

In closing, or perhaps I should say, in opening the door to your journey into PCM, I would like to tell you a personal story of how the quality of my life has been positively affected by my ongoing and, hopefully, never-ending study and practice of PCM. I am what some people would consider a happy-go-lucky and cheery person, who likes to have a great deal of fun, adventure, playful relationships, creative thinking, and action opportunities in my daily life. In other words, I have a great deal of Rebel personality that drives how I view, inter-act with, and react to the world. The significant men in my life—my father, my husband, my brother—and the major women as well—my mother and daughter—do not share Rebel with me as their primary personality type. As a consequence, for most of my life I was puzzled and sometimes angered at the way in which they talked about things. To me, everything they said seemed to be about right versus wrong, good versus evil. In other words, everything seemed like a judgment, and it drove me crazy. As a Rebel, I hardly knew how to think and talk in those terms, at least most of the time, and I considered it harsh and judgmental in the most negative sense of those words. What I learned through my PCM studies is that I simply was not aware of or understanding of their primary personality type—that of Persister. As you will learn, people with a strong Persister personality experi-ence and must describe the world in what I now know to be a very important and strong values-based way. This realization, which I acquired only through studying the personality types of PCM, opened my ears to hear these words as the words of strongly committed, moral people, who have the convictions to make things right and change the world, when they get a chance!

My life is enjoyable and makes so much more sense now that I have had PCM to help me sort out my relationships with family members and the many thousands of people I encounter and work with each year as a university professor and international educa-tional consultant. So now it is time for you to begin your studies. Learn well and enjoy the lessons this book has to teach—lessons that have the potential to enrich and possibly change forever your life and the lives of those you love.

Jacqueline S. Thousand, Ph.D.
College of Education
California State University, San Marcos

REFERENCE

Pauley, C., Pauley, J.F., & Pauley, J.A. (2000). Passing the torch. In R.A. Villa and J.S. Thousand (Eds.), *Restructuring for caring and effective education: Piecing the puzzle together* (2nd ed., pp. 590–601). Baltimore: Paul H. Brookes Publishing Co.

ACKNOWLEDGMENTS

First and foremost, we are grateful to and respectful of Taibi Kahler, Ph.D., for his genius and his discoveries in personality theory and for his ability to communicate them in an easily understood, practical system for viewing interpersonal relationships. We are especially appreciative of his friendship and his encouragement and cooperation in helping us write this book. Dr. Kahler has had a profound impact on people and organizations through the application of his Process Communication Model (PCM) to management, psychotherapy, and interpersonal communication. It is an equally powerful tool in the educational arena. The concepts of Dr. Kahler's system, Process Communication, have improved our lives and the lives of hundreds of thousands of others including many educators. Our goal in writing this book is to enable educators to reach every student in order to increase academic achievement, reduce classroom disruptions and school violence, and make the school day a rewarding experience for students and teachers.

We greatly appreciate the talents of Clinton Powell, who contributed most of the artwork. His sketches illustrate the concepts of Process Communication, making them more easily understood and making the book more reader friendly.

We acknowledge Kathryn Smith, Ed.D., Adjunct Professor at the University of Virginia; and Mary Jane Jackson, Ed.D., Adjunct Professor at Trinity College in Washington, D.C. They contributed extensively to the organization of the book. They also suggested ideas for the content of several chapters, wrote parts of two chapters, and spent many hours providing feedback. In addition, they provided case studies documenting the positive results their graduate students obtained when they applied the concepts of Process Communication in their classes.

We are grateful to Michael Gilbert, Ph.D., Director of Doctoral Research in the Department of Educational and Community Leadership, Central Michigan University, for his support and guidance while we were writing the book, and for his review and suggestions.

We want to acknowledge Maurice Zeeman, Ph.D., for his feedback and editing of several chapters. We are grateful to Okie Wolfe, Ph.D., Executive Director of the Management, Teaching, and Learning Styles Institute at Lincoln Memorial University, Harrogate, Tennessee, for her suggested correlation of learning styles to personality types.

We thank all of the educators and students who agreed to be interviewed so that we could get an accurate picture of their school experiences and their attitudes toward learning and teaching. Their frankness and willingness to share enabled us to present an accurate picture of each type of student and to document the results of the strategies recommended in this book. We also acknowledge the teachers and educators who shared with us their stories and experiences: Raquel Alcaraz, Nicole Crutchfield, Merle Cuttitta, Marcia Fineman, Maria Gowallis, Marie-Lousie Halbert, Beth Hulfish, Carol Knudson, Anne Lortie, Mary Minner, Molly O'Brien, Melissa Richards, Myra Rosen, Joseph Rowe, Peyton Taylor, Tiffani Turner, and Virginia Weinstock.

To Dr. Taibi Kahler for his genius, his friendship, and his discoveries
that are improving the lives of millions of people

INTRODUCTION

The concepts of the Process Communication Model (PCM) were developed by Taibi Kahler, Ph.D., and were initially used by psychiatrists and psychologists with their patients. In 1978, Dr. Kahler adapted the concepts of PCM for behavioral use when he was invited by the National Aeronautics and Space Administration (NASA) to sit in on the astronaut selection interviews. Subsequently, while continuing to serve as an advisor to NASA, chief executive officers of major corporations asked him to apply the concepts of PCM to management and team building. Dr. Kahler published *The Mastery of Management* (Kahler Communications, Inc., 2000), which describes PCM in detail.

Joseph and Judith Pauley were first exposed to PCM as a management tool in 1987. They were impressed by the effectiveness of the concepts in their professional lives and began applying them in meetings to maintain a positive relationship with everyone on the school team as they advocated for their daughter, a young woman with Down syndrome.

One day, they received a telephone call from their daughter's special education teacher asking for a parent conference. The teacher was frustrated by their daughter's behaviors and was experiencing a daily power struggle that was exhausting for both of them.

During the Pauleys' meeting with the teacher, they described the PCM concepts and how they could be used to reach their daughter. Two weeks later, the teacher called to report that their daughter's rebellious behaviors had stopped and invited the Pauleys to do an in-service training session on PCM for the school. She added that she was no longer tired at the end of the day. That meeting led to many others, and the authors increased their efforts to help educators apply the concepts to help reach and teach every student. Subsequently, Judith Pauley began using the concepts in her high school chemistry and physics classes with dramatic improvement in student achievement. As a result, she was named science teacher of the year three times.

Dr. Dianne Bradley has worked extensively in school settings as a general educator, special educator and guidance counselor, and system wide as a teacher trainer and supervisor. She first discovered PCM in her job as a compliance specialist, where she mediated with parents who were unhappy with the way in which their children's individualized education programs (IEPs) were implemented. After taking a 3-day course in PCM, her success rate in mediations soared to 99%. She received her certification in PCM training and has since pursued her interest in applying the concepts to the educational arena. As an adjunct college professor and student teaching supervisor, she has used the ideas described in this book in teaching and mentoring new teachers. She has written several articles on using PCM in the classroom and trains teachers and administrators in using these concepts in the school setting.

Note from the authors: We have gained much wisdom from teachers across the country with whom we have shared the concepts of the Process Communication Model. Educators who successfully implemented PCM in their classrooms supplied many of the stories in this book. We have tried to write a user-friendly book that contains specific strategies that you can use to reach each of your students. We hope that by applying these concepts with your students, they will learn more and behave better. We also hope that by using these ideas, you will experience less stress and enjoy teaching more!

CHAPTER 1

Welcome to your classroom. You are the ringmaster for 30 diverse learners. How are you going to teach in order to reach them all? What are you going to do to maintain their interest and enthusiasm to learn? Many teachers have found the concepts of the Process Communication Model (PCM) very useful in reaching every student and in keeping them motivated. Others have never heard of PCM. This book is for all of you.

What is PCM, and how can it help teachers reach out to students who have different needs and personality types? PCM is a powerful communication tool developed by Dr. Taibi Kahler, a clinical psychologist in Little Rock, Arkansas. Briefly stated, PCM provides a way for teachers and others to communicate with and motivate people by shifting to their preferred frame of reference. To categorize these frames of reference, Dr. Kahler (1982) identified six different personality types based on individuals' perceptions of the world (i.e., how they take in and process information). He found that each person prefers to communicate in different ways depending on his or her personality type (Kahler, 2000). In order to communicate effectively, then, Kahler suggests that people learn to speak the "languages" that other people prefer. His research shows that doing so will significantly increase the likelihood that the content of their message is "heard" and acted on. Dr. Kahler compares this to a person traveling to a foreign country. If residents of the foreign country do not speak the language of the traveler, then the traveler must speak their language if he or she wants to be understood. Dr. Kahler has identified six different "languages" people speak and six different ways people are motivated based on their personality type. In addition, he found that individuals of each personality type have predictable patterns of distress when their needs are not met positively.

According to the PCM research, everyone is one of these six personality types (Kahler, 1974). None of these types is any better or worse than any other, and each type has its strengths and weaknesses. Frequently, these weaknesses are seen when people become distressed because they have not gotten their motivational needs met positively. When people are in distress, they are not capable of thinking clearly; they will mask their true feelings and will display predictable negative behaviors. Usually, this results in miscommunication. This book focuses on how teachers can make positive interventions or even prevent these behaviors from occurring.

THE SIX PERSONALITY TYPES

Dr. Kahler (1974) has identified these six personality types:

- Reactors
- Workaholics
- Persisters
- Dreamers
- Rebels
- Promoters

The characteristics and perceptions of each of the six types are shown in Table 1.1 (Kahler 1982, 1996). The percentage of each type represented in the North American population is shown in Figure 1.1 (Kahler, 1982, 1996).

Reactors are people of great compassion, sensitivity, and warmth. They perceive the world through their emotions. They feel first—about people, places and things—and want others to share their feelings. They have great interpersonal skills and care about others. They like people and want to be liked in return. In fact, they need to hear that people like them not for anything they have done but for who they are. They are very good at nurturing others. Compassion is their currency. As a result, many Reactors become elementary school teachers or special education teachers.

Table 1.1. Characteristics and perceptions of types

Type	Character strengths	Perception
Reactor	Compassionate, sensitive, warm	Emotions
Workaholic	Responsible, logical, organized	Thoughts
Persister	Conscientious, dedicated, observant	Opinions
Dreamer	Reflective, imaginative, calm	Inaction
Rebel	Creative, spontaneous, playful	Reactions
Promoter	Resourceful, adaptable, charming	Actions

From Kahler, T. (1982). *Personality pattern inventory validation studies.* Little Rock, AR: Kahler Communications, Inc., and Kahler, T. (1996). *Personality pattern inventory.* Little Rock, AR: Kahler Communications, Inc.; adapted by permission.

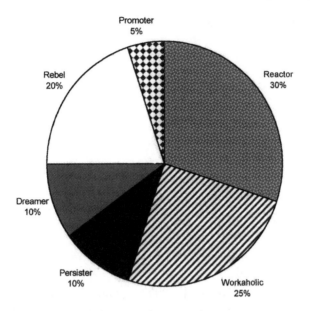

Figure 1.1. Percentages of personality types as they occur in North America. (From Kahler, T. [1982]. *Personality pattern inventory validation studies.* Little Rock, AR: Kahler Communications, Inc., and Kahler, T. [1996]. *Personality pattern inventory.* Little Rock, AR: Kahler Communications, Inc.; adapted by permission.)

Workaholics are people who are responsible, logical, and organized. They perceive the world through their thoughts. They value facts and view the world by identifying and categorizing people and things. They want people to think *with* them. Because they are information oriented, they believe the problems of the world can be solved if they just get enough information. Workaholics like to discuss options and to hear that people appreciate their ability to think clearly, come up with good ideas, and do a good job. Logic is their currency. Many middle school and high school teachers are Workaholics.

Persisters are conscientious, dedicated, and observant. They perceive the world through their opinions; they take in information and very quickly form opinions about everyone and everything. Once they have formed an opinion, it is difficult to get them to change their beliefs. They are committed to loyalty, quality, values, standards, and

their mission of helping others succeed. They may not care if anyone likes them as long as their dedication and commitment are respected and appreciated. They want everyone to achieve to his or her full potential, and, as a result, many Persisters become teachers. Values are their currency. Many middle school and high school teachers are Persisters.

Dreamers are reflective, imaginative, and calm. They conceptualize things in ways that are different from how people of other types conceptualize things. They want to be told what is expected of them and then prefer to be left alone to carry out instructions. They take in information by reflection. This means that although they probably understand the information presented, they will reflect on it and not act on it unless given specific, concise instructions. They value direction. If they are engaged in something, they tend to continue to do it until told to do something else. Imagination is their currency. A few Dreamers become teachers, but not very many.

Rebels are spontaneous, creative, playful, and fun. They like to have a good time. They perceive the world through reactions—that is, their likes and dislikes. They are energetic and may be artistic or musical. In fact, music, art, physical education, computer classes, and extracurricular activities help Rebels get through the school day. They prize spontaneity and creativity. Humor is their currency. Some Rebels become teachers, but not very many.

Promoters are resourceful, charming, and adaptable. They perceive the world by experiencing situations and by making things happen. They prize adaptability and self-sufficiency and like a lot of excitement in their lives. Charm is their currency, and they thrive on quick rewards. They are very direct and are action oriented. They want to do things *now* and get right to the bottom line—no working 30 years for a gold watch for them! (In the classroom, Promoters would not want to wait even a grading period for a grade or a week for a sticker or free time). They want their reward today, this week, or this month. As a result, almost none of them become teachers.

THE STRUCTURE OF PERSONALITY

Two other aspects of personality types should be discussed before getting into the mechanics of how to use PCM as a tool.

The Language of Personality

First, although each person is predominantly one of these types, he or she has parts of all six with varying degrees of dominance. To understand this concept, picture a six-floor condominium. It is theorized that people are born with their base personality type already established. The order of the arrangement of the other personality types in their personality structure is determined by environmental factors, however. This arrangement is usually developed in a person's life up to age 6 or 7, at which time the order does not change again throughout his or her lifetime (Stansbury, 1990).

Because each person has parts of all six personality types in his or her personality structure, everyone has the potential to speak the language of all six types. These languages are based on how each personality type takes in and processes information and are discussed in greater detail in the perception section that follows. Each person speaks one or two of these languages fluently but is not as articulate in the others because some parts of an individual's personality tend to be better developed than other parts. Consequently, it requires more energy for an individual to gain access to those parts, in other words, to speak the languages that are preferred by the personality types that are not well developed in that person.

Students whose best-developed characteristics match the best-developed personality types in their teachers would be expected to do well in school. For example, in Figure 1.2 the teacher's base personality is Persister. This particular teacher has Workaholic well developed on the second floor, Reactor fairly well developed on the third floor, Dreamer not well developed on the fourth floor, Promoter not well developed on the fifth floor, and Rebel very poorly developed on the sixth floor. Teachers who have this personality structure will be quite effective teaching Persisters and Workaholics,

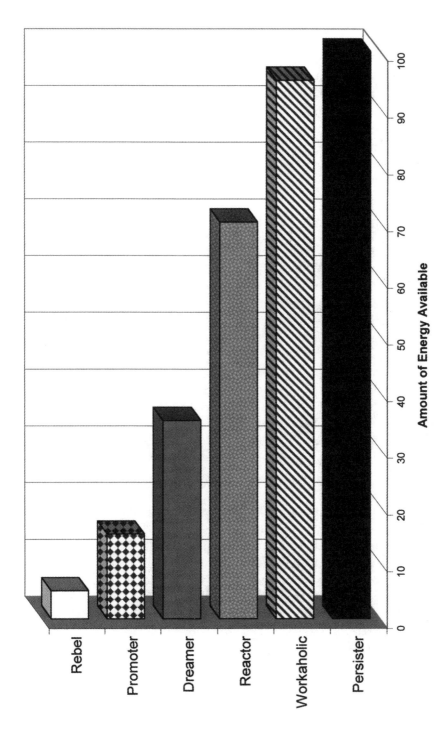

Figure 1.2. Personality structure of a typical secondary school teacher. (From Kahler, T. [1982]. *Personality pattern inventory validation studies*. Little Rock, AR: Kahler Communications, Inc., and Kahler, T. [1996]. *Personality pattern inventory*. Little Rock, AR: Kahler Communications, Inc.; adapted by permission.)

and will be reasonably effective teaching Reactors. They will not be effective teaching Dreamers, Promoters, and Rebels in the classroom, however, unless they learn how to speak the languages of these three types of students.

A Rebel with the personality structure in Figure 1.3 will be at risk in this teacher's class. No one is to blame for this. A teacher with a personality structure similar to the one in Figure 1.2 probably does not know how to speak the language of a student with a personality structure such as the student in Figure 1.3. Conversely, a student with the personality structure of the student in Figure 1.3 almost certainly does not know how to speak the language of the teacher in Figure 1.2. As a result, they tune each other out and do not hear the content of what the other is saying. In this instance the content is ignored, and there is no communication, no discussion, and no learning. It is these students who often get labeled (and mislabeled) as inattentive, as having an emotional disturbance, and as acting out. The solution is for teachers to determine the perceptions each student uses and to speak to him or her in the appropriate language (i.e., the individual's perception). Remember that there can be no learning if students cannot "hear" the content. They cannot "hear" the content unless teachers speak their language. The goal is to facilitate the learning process by connecting perception to perception.

Let's look at another example. Figure 1.4 is a very common profile of an elementary school teacher. This teacher is a base Reactor with Workaholic well developed on the second floor and Persister fairly well developed on the third floor. This particular teacher has Dreamer not well developed on the fourth floor, Promoter not well developed on the fifth floor, and Rebel very poorly developed on the sixth floor. A teacher with this profile would do well teaching Reactors and Workaholics and reasonably well teaching Persisters but might have difficulty teaching Rebels, Promoters, and Dreamers. A student with the personality structure in Figure 1.3 also will be at risk in this teacher's class. Again, this is no one's fault. The teacher is doing the best he or she can with the tools that are available at the time, and the student is doing the best he or she can. The good news is that if the teacher will learn the language of the student, the student can and will learn.

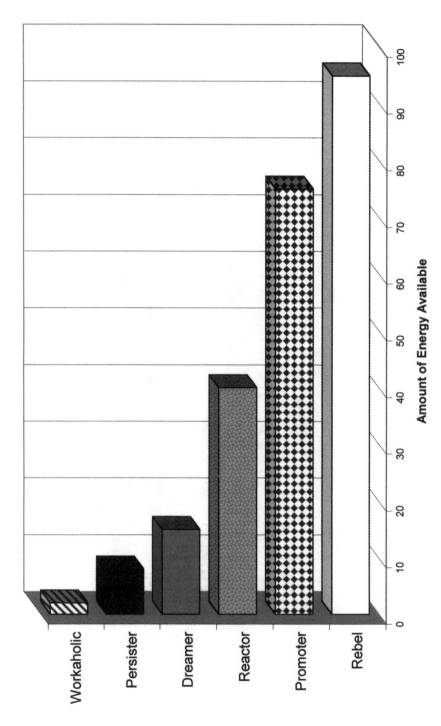

Figure 1.3. Personality structure of a Rebel student at risk. (From Kahler, T. [1982]. *Personality pattern inventory validation studies.* Little Rock, AR: Kahler Communications, Inc., and Kahler, T. [1996]. *Personality pattern inventory.* Little Rock, AR: Kahler Communications, Inc.; adapted by permission.)

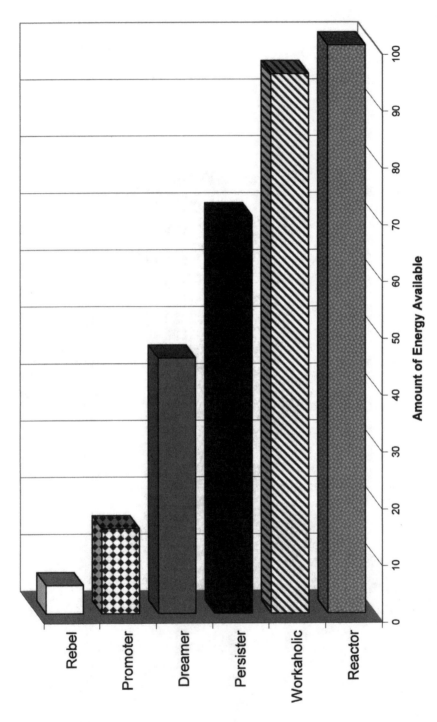

Figure 1.4. Personality structure of a typical elementary school teacher. (From Kahler, T. [1982]. *Personality pattern inventory validation studies*. Little Rock, AR: Kahler Communications, Inc.; and Kahler, T. [1996]. *Personality pattern inventory*. Little Rock, AR: Kahler Communications, Inc.; adapted by permission.)

Phases

Second, it is useful to understand the concept of *phase*. As North Americans go through life, two thirds of them experience a "phase change" (Kahler, 1974, 1995). When this happens, they move to the next floor in their personality structure and essentially operate with a new driving force (Kahler, 1995). While experiencing a phase change (phasing) people very often exhibit intense negative behaviors associated with their current personality type. After a person has completed a phase change, he or she will have new motivational needs and a new sequence of negative behaviors. This new phase lasts from 2 years to a lifetime.

Phasing might also be a contributing factor in many situations in life: divorce, burnout, and mid-life crisis, to name a few. When people experience a phase change, they retain and strengthen the positive attributes and behaviors associated with past phases, and many aspects of their personality remain the same. For example, their character strengths and their preferences for interacting with others are always with them. Their favorite channel and the most well-developed parts of their personality remain the same. So does their preferred learning style, their perception of the world, and working styles (e.g., in groups, alone, with one other person). The concept of phasing helps to explain how individuals can be the same people throughout their lives even though their dreams, aspirations, careers, and personal goals may change (Kahler 1995). When people experience a phase change, they experience changes in motivation and in the way in which they handle distress. The following story illustrates the impact of phase on one teacher's life.

A TEACHER'S STORY

I was born a Persister (see Figure 1.5). As a Persister I learned very quickly that life was a serious place. I developed a sense of direction, mission, and conviction and was motivated by working hard and dedicating myself to causes. Values, beliefs, dedication, commitment, respect, and community service were important to me. I was in the Boy Scouts, was an altar server at church, and was on the school patrol. This dedication to causes has been a continuous theme throughout my life.

When I was 10 years old, my father injured his back and was disabled for the rest of his life. Left without a source of family income, I quickly assumed that it was up to me to support the family; therefore, I took on jobs such as weeding gardens, mowing lawns, shoveling snow, and running paper routes. Persisters are conscientious; I remember waking up nights, afraid that my family would starve because I could not earn enough money to support them. I spent a lot of time in distress and began to criticize and attack others for lacking commitment and dedication. Finally, I dealt with my fear and moved to the next floor of my personality condominium (i.e., the Workaholic part of my personality structure). I had completed my phase change. I was still a Persister, but now I was operating in a Workaholic mode.

In a Workaholic phase I began to be more responsible, logical, and organized. I was still conscientious and dedicated and continued to work hard for something I believed in. I was still motivated by being recognized for my work. But an additional motivator, time, began to drive me. Suddenly, I had a compulsion to be on time for everything. Being late or turning in an assignment late was anathema to me. At this time I began to excel in mathematics, and I scored in the 99th percentile on a national achievement test. This gained me some national attention, and I began college as a mathematics major.

After several years in a Workaholic phase, I began to get depressed because things were not working out as I thought they should. I was working very hard, yet we remained poor. I was supporting my father, yet his health continued to deteriorate. I looked after my mother, yet she experienced a series of accidents and operations. I began to criticize and attack others for not thinking clearly and working hard enough. Finally, I dealt with my depression, and I moved to the next floor in my condominium—my Rebel floor.

What a change in my life! I began to have more fun than I ever had. I suddenly developed a nonconformist side of my personality and was expelled from college for my behavior. I then enrolled in a teacher's college near my home. Naturally, I enrolled as a mathematics major. Although I was still very good in math, the logic of it no longer appealed to me. I went out for the college soccer team, and after about a week I decided that my chemistry and physics labs were interfering with my soccer practices. I figured that if I wanted to make the team, I had better switch majors. Overnight I became an English major.

Because of my Persister and Workaholic strengths, I understood the structure of language and had a good background in grammar. In high school I had worked very hard to master the art of writing and, as a result, I was good at it. I liked to write poetry, and I liked to act in plays and sing in musicals; therefore, I thought being an English major would be fun. I also thought it would be fun to teach kids to love plays, books, and poetry. During my 4 years in college as an English major I wrote for the college paper; acted in drama club plays and musicals; and was able to play on the soccer, basketball, and baseball teams. Because of my Persister drive, I became editor of the college paper and captain of the soccer team my senior year. College was fun.

After graduation I taught English and coached in a middle school in a town about 10 miles from my home. I liked teaching English, and I liked interacting with the kids. I used to do a lot of fun things in the classroom to keep my students interested, such as acting out stories we were reading and writing poems, songs, and short stories. I would also have contests or relay races to see which student or team would be the first to answer my questions correctly.

To further maintain my students' attention, I sometimes took a quarter out of my pocket, placed it on my thumb, and started flipping it while I asked questions. One of the questions was the "two-bit question." When the students answered that question correctly I would flip the quarter across the room to them. Because the students never knew which question was the key one, they stayed alert through the entire class. One of the boys in the class, Tommy, was the class clown and always acted out. The other students did not know how smart he was until they saw him in action in this class. He was very energized and frequently won the quarter for answering the "two-bit question" correctly. It wasn't the monetary value of the quarter that energized everyone. Rather, it was the competition for a prize or reward. Soon, the principal began assigning the "troublemakers" and underachievers to my classes. For some reason they were successful in my classes.

I remained in a Rebel phase for nearly 15 years, and then my wife and I were blessed with a daughter who had Down syndrome. After her birth, I began to develop more compassion, sensitivity, and warmth. I began to feel about people and things. In a Rebel phase I wanted to do my own thing, and I bristled at restrictions and at being told what I had to do. I did not care what others thought of me as long as they left me alone to teach the way I wanted to teach. Suddenly, all of that

changed. I had experienced another phase change. Now I wanted to nurture and protect our daughter and to help her be all that she could be. I began to care what people thought about me. I wanted them to like me, and I began to develop close friendships with people. I became acutely aware of people with disabilities, and I decided I wanted to help them, too. Because of my Persister base I believed I could help them best by becoming a special education teacher, so I changed careers again.

I was in a Reactor phase, but I was still a base Persister. My (phase) need at that time was to help people, especially loved ones. My original (base) need fueled my conviction. Consequently, our daughter became my primary cause and I began to advocate for her. As I learned more, I became an advocate for inclusive education. I got politically active in an effort to educate our school board, our county council, and our central administration about the benefits of inclusion. I cared about people with special needs becoming integral members of society. I was indeed a Persister in a Reactor phase.

PERCEPTIONS

The importance of speaking the language of each student has been discussed previously. But how can a teacher determine the preferred language or perception of each student? One way is for teachers to listen for verbal cues that indicate perceptions—how each student takes in and processes information (see Table 1.1). For example, Reactors perceive the world through their *emotions.* They take in people and things through feeling for and about them, and they want others to share feelings with them. Workaholics perceive the world through their *thoughts.* They are data oriented and seek information. They want people to think with them. Persisters perceive the world through their *opinions.* When they get information, they very quickly form a value judgment. They expect people to ask their opinions of things. Dreamers perceive the world through *inaction.* They tend not to undertake tasks until someone tells them what to do. Rebels perceive the world through their *reactions.* They let everyone know what they like and what they do not like, usually without regard to the conse-

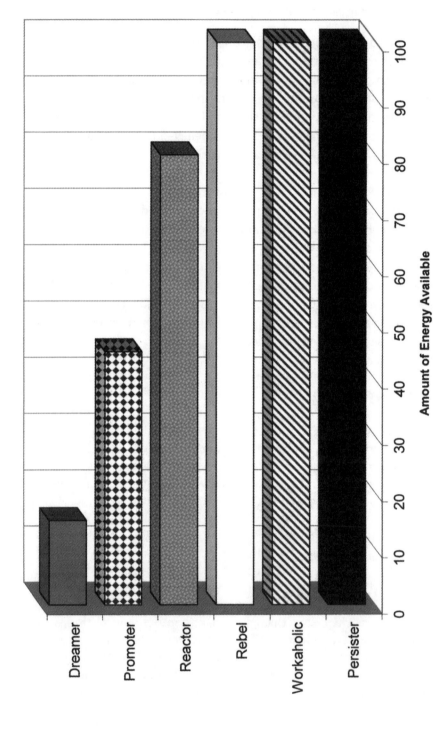

Figure 1.5. Personality structure of one teacher who has experienced four phase changes. (From Kahler, T. [1982]. *Personality pattern inventory validation studies.* Little Rock, AR: Kahler Communications, Inc., and Kahler, T. [1996]. *Personality pattern inventory.* Little Rock, AR: Kahler Communications, Inc.; adapted by permission.)

quences. Promoters perceive the world through *actions*. They act first, usually without thinking. They want people to act with them, and they get antsy when people discuss things for too long.

The language associated with each perception is very distinctive. By listening for these verbal cues, teachers can determine which language they should use with which student.

Emotions

Teachers can listen for "I feel"; "In my heart";s and references to family, friends, emotions, love, happiness, caring, compassion, and harmony. When they hear these cues, teachers can respond with, "We care about," "We appreciate your concern," "In our hearts," and "Let's remember how people feel about." They can also support the student with compassionate statements and can reaffirm them with consideration for the feelings of others.

Thoughts

Teachers should listen for "I think," "The facts are," and "Our options include." They should also listen for references to data, information, logic, fairness, categories, time, agendas, and order. When teachers hear these cues, they can respond with, "What do you think about," "What facts support," "Do you have an idea that," and "What options do you." Teachers also should ask questions to elicit factual information and encourage logical thinking: "Who," "What," "When," "Where," and "How."

Opinions

Teachers should listen for "In my opinion"; "We should"; "I believe"; and references to respect, values, commitment, trust, mission, dedication, morals, and concepts of right and wrong. When they hear these verbal cues, teachers can respond with, "In your opinion, should we," "Do you believe we should," and "What is your opinion." Teachers can also ask questions to elicit values and beliefs.

Inaction (Reflection)

Teachers can listen for "We need time to reflect on this," "I don't want to antagonize anyone," and "Let's not make waves." Other cues might be references to needing time to consider situations, not wanting to offend people, not being too aggressive, and the importance of one's own space and privacy. Teachers can respond with, "Take your time on this one," "Let's each of us go at our own pace on this," and "Let's not jump to conclusions." Teachers can also use softened imperatives that give students permission to take time to ponder, reflect, and consider what to do in a calm, inoffensive manner.

Reactions (Likes and Dislikes)

Teachers can listen for phrases such as "I like," "I hate this," "Great!," "This is the pits!," "I want," "I can't stand," and references that indicate the student is responding to things with likes and dislikes. When they hear these cues teachers can respond with, "Yeah, I don't like that either"; "That's awesome—I'm with you"; "It's the pits!"; and can make lively comments, use humor, and keep things upbeat.

Actions

Teachers should listen for "Bottom line"; "Enough talk"; "best shot"; "Make it happen"; "Just do it!"; and references to initiative, action, immediacy, adaptability, and the end justifying the means. When they hear these verbal cues, teachers can respond with, "I hear you," "You want action," "Let's do it," "Ten minutes to get this done," "Rock and roll time," and "Give it your best shot." Teachers should use imperatives with action verbs and should be energetic and charismatic.

LANGUAGE IN OPERATION

To understand how the language of the six personality types differs, let's look at how each type would tell the story of *Goldilocks and the Three Bears.*

Reactor (Emotions)

"Once upon a time, there was a little girl named Goldilocks. She was a sweet little girl who was called Goldilocks because she had beautiful blonde hair that shone like gold in the sunlight. Looking nice was important to her because she felt good when she looked her best. Therefore, she brushed her hair every day. She always felt very comfortable walking in the woods. She could smell the beautiful flowers and breathe the clean fresh air. Life was wonderful."

Workaholic (Thoughts)

"Once upon a time, there was a little girl named Goldilocks. She was 8 years old, stood 3 feet 6 inches tall, and weighed 60 pounds. She was called Goldilocks because she had blonde hair. One day, she went walking in the woods. She got lost and wandered aimlessly for 4 hours. Eventually, she came to a small house. The house was two stories tall and was about 20 feet long by 14 feet wide. On the north

side ground floor there were three windows about 4 feet tall and 30 inches wide. On the second floor there were three windows about the same size."

Persister (Opinions)

"Once upon a time there was a little girl named Goldilocks. She was 8 years old but was small for her age. She liked to walk in the woods alone. In my opinion her parents should not have allowed her to go walking in the woods without them because there were wild bears in the area. Walking in the woods in bear country is dangerous at any time, but especially so for a little girl alone. Because she was careless

and did not pay attention to where she was going, she lost her way. After wandering aimlessly for 4 hours she became tired. She probably would have given up except that she very luckily happened upon a small cottage."

Dreamer (Inaction)

"Once upon a time there was a little girl named Goldilocks. (Pause) Umm. One day she went walking in the woods and (pause) umm . . . she got lost. She walked around until she . . . umm (pause) found a little cottage. She was tired and hungry and went in. (Pause) Umm. No one was home, but on the table there were three bowls of porridge. (Pause) She tasted them. (Pause) Umm. One bowl was too hot. (Pause) Ummm. One was too cold. (Pause) Ummm. The third one was just right and she ate it . . . ."

Rebel (Reactions)

"Once upon a time there was this little girl named Goldilocks. She was an awesome kid who loved to walk in the woods because she always had fun there. There were some huge trees that seemed to go

clear to the sky. The woods were awesome too—trees, flowers, rabbits, squirrels. They even had bears. Lions and tigers and bears, oh my. One day when she was walking in the woods she got lost. She wandered around for a while until she came to this cool little cottage. She was beat and hungry so she went in. On the table she spied three bowls of porridge. She tried the first one, but it burned her mouth. She tried the second, but it was too cold. Have you ever had to eat cold porridge? Yuck!!"

Promoter (Actions)

"Once upon a time there was a little girl named Goldilocks. She walked in the woods all the time. One day she went walking and got lost. She stumbled around for a while and finally came to a small cabin. She knocked on the door, but no one answered. She yelled out, "Is anybody home?" No answer. Finally, she went in. On the kitchen table she saw three bowls of porridge. She tasted the first one. It was too hot. She tasted the second one. It was too cold. She tasted the third one. It was just right, and she ate the whole bowl. She was tired, too. She went upstairs and saw three beds. She climbed on the first one. It was too hard. She climbed down, walked to the second one, and sat

on it. It was too soft. She got up and went to the third one. She lay down on it. It was just right and she fell asleep . . . . "

WRITTEN CUES

Students also write according to their perception of the world. Therefore, teachers can look for clues to the students' perceptions in their written assignments. Reactors will write about people and will use feeling words. Workaholics will give a lot of factual information. Persisters will imply or give opinions of events they describe and may use terms such as "I believe" or "in my opinion." Dreamers will write very concise papers with very little descriptive language. They may use imaginative approaches to homework assignments such as writing a poem to illustrate a concept. Rebels will use their creativity to do assignments that appeal to them and may use very colorful language to describe their reactions to the topic they are writing about. Promoters will use a lot of action verbs in their papers and may write about exciting things.

MOTIVATIONAL NEEDS

How can teachers use their knowledge of personality types to ensure that they reach every student every day? One way is to use this understanding to motivate students. PCM research has shown that in addition to a preferred perception, each of the six personality types has a favorite channel of communication, and each has different motivational needs that must be met (Kahler, 2000). If students' needs are met positively, they are much more likely to react positively to their teachers and the learning environment. If students' needs are not met positively, they may get into distress and do things to get negative attention. What they do will vary depending on their personality type. For example, some students may act the part of the class clown, throw chairs, hit or kick their classmates, or swear at their teachers. Others may create negative drama by manipulating fellow students or teachers. Kahler (1974) and others describe these offensive behaviors as the means by which people get their motivational needs met negatively. The distress behaviors for each specific type are discussed in Chapters 9 and 11.

When people get into distress, their ability to think is impaired, and they almost always will experience negative learning situations and make life miserable for those around them. Research and experience using PCM in school settings show that if students get their motivational needs met positively in school, these negative behaviors will be greatly reduced or completely disappear. When teachers help students get their motivational needs met positively, the students will have a better attitude toward school, will learn more, and will act out less in class (Bradley & Smith, 1999; Gilbert, 1992; Gilbert & Bailey, 2000). A bonus for teachers is that they will be less tired at the end of the day (Jackson & Pauley, 1999).

How can teachers motivate every student individually? Each of the six types has different motivational needs (see Table 1.2):

- Reactor students need **personal recognition** and **sensory stimulation**. They like an environment that feels comfortable and nest-like. They also respond to soothing music, earth-tone colors, and pleasant smells. They like to talk about people, especially those who are close to them—their parents, their siblings, their friends, or their children or spouses. They need to be appreciated just because they are nice people. In short, they need unconditional acceptance. They like sincere compliments about their looks, their clothes, their jewelry, their home, and so forth. Reactor students may work for A's, but only because they want to please

Table 1.2. Motivational needs of personality types

Type	Needs
Reactor	Recognition of person Sensory stimulation
Workaholic	Recognition for ability to think clearly, work Time structure
Persister	Recognition for work Recognition for convictions and commitment
Dreamer	Solitude
Rebel	Playful contact
Promoter	Incidence, excitement

From Kahler, T. (1982). *Personality pattern inventory validation studies.* Little Rock, AR: Kahler Communications, Inc., and Kahler, T. (1996). *Personality pattern inventory.* Little Rock, AR: Kahler Communications, Inc.; adapted by permission.

their parents or their teachers. Grades are not their primary motivation.

- Workaholic students need to be recognized for their **ability to think clearly** and for their **hard work**. They need to hear "Good job." "Well done." "Good idea." **Time structure** also is important to them. They need to know when assignments are due and how the day will be structured. They work for A's because when they receive them they are recognized for their work.

- Persister students also need to hear "Good job," or "Good idea" and to have their **work recognized**. It is even more important to them that people respect their convictions and **commitment** to standards and ask their opinions of things, however. Persister students work for A's and frequently help other students with their work.

- Dreamer students' primary motivation is **solitude**. In order to function well in school, they need their own private time and private space. They do not participate in lengthy discussions. They prefer teachers who tell them concisely what to do, show them how to do it, and then leave them alone to accomplish the task. Grades are not their primary motivation.

- Rebel students need **playful contact.** They like to have fun and are not necessarily motivated by getting good grades. They like to be on stage in the classroom, and they appreciate teachers who are relaxed and who have fun with them. They learn best from teachers who include fun things in their lessons.

- Promoter students are motivated by **excitement**. They like to have something going on all the time. They are thrill seekers who need action and movement. They get bored when people talk a lot. For them action is where it's at.

Rebels, Promoters, and Dreamers are the students who have the most difficulty in school. These are typically the least-developed personalities among educators, and many teachers do not speak these students' language and have great difficulty motivating those who have these dominant personality types. These students are often seen by their teachers as unmotivated or as having attention or behavior disorders or even learning disabilities.

When teachers are aware of the needs of each of the types, they can build in methods for helping each type of student get their needs met. For instance, they can greet Reactors at the door and tell them how nice they look or how glad they are to see them. They can recognize Persisters and Workaholics for their hard work and great ideas. Games and/or jokes can be built into many lessons to grab the atten-

Table 1.3. How four channels elicit communication and miscommunication

Channel	Dialogue	Communication	Miscommunication
Directive	Tell me where you are going.	I'm going to the office.	Do you mean you want me to tell you where I am going?
Requestive	Where are you going?	To the office.	Do you mean you want me to tell you where I am going?
Nurturative	That's a beautiful sweater. You always look so stylish.	Thank you.	Same sweater I've been wearing all week.
Emotive	Hey, awesome shirt, dude!	Yeah, it's cool, huh?	There's nothing wrong with my shirt.

From Kahler, T. (1979). *Process therapy in brief.* Little Rock, AR: Human Development Publications; adapted by permission.

tion of Rebels and Promoters, and teachers can make sure that Dreamers get some solitude during the day. (See Chapter 10 for further ideas on meeting individual needs in the classroom.)

CHANNELS OF COMMUNICATION

Another key to communicating successfully with each type of student is understanding the four channels of communication that are preferred by the six different personality types (see Table 1.3). These channels are like a CB radio. If the teacher is on channel 9 and the student is on channel 7, they are not going to hear each other.

An analogy is a room with four doors. Let's assume that one of the doors is the student's favorite door and he or she uses it most of the time. Let's also assume that one of the doors is boarded up and the student never uses it, and that the student only occasionally uses the other two doors. If the teacher only uses her or his favorite door when teaching and that door is the one that the student never uses, it is likely the student will not hear accurately and that the teacher

and student will miscommunicate. If teachers want to ensure that every student hears them, they periodically must shift to the favorite door (i.e., the channel) of each student during class.

What are these four channels, and which ones work best with which types?

1. The **Directive channel** lets the listener know exactly what is expected and is given as a clear directive. For example, "Tell me where you are going." The Directive channel works best with Dreamers who need clear direction and with Promoters who need to know the bottom line.

2. The **Requestive channel** asks a question and is responded to best by Workaholics and Persisters. These personality types already know what they are supposed to do and prefer to be asked questions. It sounds like this: "Where are you going?"

3. Reactors who like soft tones and gentleness prefer the **Nurturative channel.** "That's a beautiful sweater. You always look so stylish."

4. There is also a channel for the Rebel that is called the **Emotive channel.** "Hey, awesome shirt, dude!" This channel helps to maintain the interest of the Rebel, who tends to become easily bored.

Because successful communication requires two people, there must be an offer and a prompt, clear response that makes sense in order for communication to take place. In the example of the Nurturative channel, a response of "Thank you" shows that the respondent accepted and acknowledged the speaker; thus, the two are communicating effectively. The response of "Same sweater I've been wearing all week" indicates that communication is not taking place and probably means that the responder is not open to the Nurturative channel.

STUDENTS AND EDUCATORS IN DISTRESS

As we have noted previously, research shows that most elementary school teachers are Reactors with Persister and Workaholic second and third (see Figure 1.4). They tend to have Rebel, Promoter, and Dreamer as their least well-developed parts. Most middle school and high school teachers are Persisters with Workaholics second or Workaholics with Persisters second, with Reactor third (see Figure 1.2). They, too, tend to have Dreamer, Rebel and Promoter as their least well-developed parts (Bailey, 1998; Gilbert, 1992, 1994, 1996). As a result of this difference in their personality structures, many teachers have difficulty reaching and teaching these three types of students. Consequently, Dreamers, Rebels, and Promoters make up a very high percentage of students who drop out of school, who are referred for diagnosis for attention-deficit/hyperactivity disorder (ADHD), who are referred for special education, and who get into difficulty with teachers and peers (Bailey, 1998; Bailey & Gilbert, 1999). Often, these students are in distress.

What happens if teachers do not get their own needs met and, consequently, respond emotionally to their students? In PCM terms, the six-floor condominium has a doorway leading to the basement, a basement, and a cellar (see Figure 1.6). Dr. Kahler has described the doorway as first-degree distress (the least amount of distress), the

The Three Degrees of Miscommunication

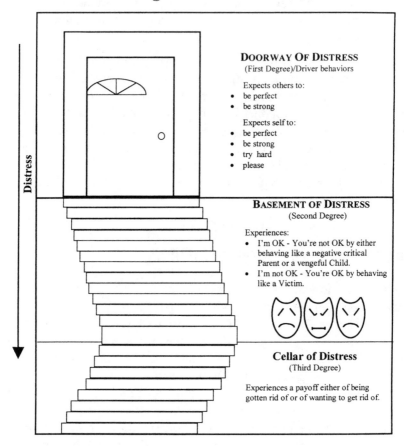

Figure 1.6. The three degrees of miscommunication. (From Kahler, T. [1979]. *Process therapy in brief.* Little Rock, AR: Human Development Publications; adapted by permission.)

basement as second-degree distress, and the cellar as third-degree distress (the most severe distress). These are sequential, and the behaviors are predictable for each personality type.

The more deeply people are distressed, the less they are capable of thinking clearly. In addition, when people are in the doorway, basement, or cellar, they mask their true feelings and reactions and invite a masked response.

This means that when a speaker is in distress he or she invites miscommunication with the listeners. For example, when a student

says, "I hate this class—it's so boring!" A teacher might assume a superior attitude and preach at the student, saying something such as, "You'll need this information later in life to get along, so you'd better pay attention." The student has successfully pulled the teacher into the doorway of distress, and a power struggle is likely to ensue where both end up in their basements. The student may act out or swear at the teacher, and the teacher may respond by sending the student to the office. Usually, these behaviors have nothing to do with the teacher who is on the receiving end. However, these differences can result in conflicts based on the different communication styles and motivational needs of educators and their students. Sometimes, these conflicts can result in both the student and the teacher becoming frustrated and perhaps even physically ill by the end of the day.

Fortunately, it need not be this way. People in distress display-ing negative behaviors are only showing symptoms of a problem of miscommunication. When teachers remember that students who behave in ways contrary to the typical teacher profile (high in Worka-holic, Persister, Reactor energy), are doing this as a function of their dominant personality type rather than willful misbehavior, the teachers can avoid getting involved in these dances of miscommu-nication (Bradley & Smith, 1999).

CONCLUSION

In a school situation, teachers, students, administrators, and parents may be of differing personality types and have different needs. Though the personality mixes make the days exciting, managing these differences in the classroom can be challenging to educators. An important thing to remember, however, is that each type and every person has strengths and can make positive contributions. Those who understand the concepts of PCM know it is in their best interest to connect with students through the perception and chan-nel associated with their base personality types and to encourage them through their phase motivational needs. Teachers need not change their personalities when they teach. They only need to be-come more fluent in a few personality type languages, so that they will be able to reach every student. When they use this information about channels, perceptions, and motivational needs to head off distress and to resolve conflicts, they are more likely to have happy, productive, and motivated students in their classrooms and to be more energetic and motivated themselves.

ROSIE REACTOR
THE FEELER

CHAPTER 2

A STUDENT'S STORY

I'm Rosie Reactor. What a beautiful morning! The sun is out, and plants are blooming everywhere. Even the little bunnies were scampering in our yard when I woke up. When everything is so lush with life, my senses are almost overwhelmed, and I'm so happy! Usually, I like to stay snuggled in my bed a few extra minutes before getting up, but today, because it was so gorgeous outside, I jumped right out of bed so I could enjoy some extra time outside before school. I brought some of the wildflowers inside to brighten up the living room and bedroom before I left.

I chose a special outfit to wear to school today. I always dress tastefully and stylishly, and I care about my appearance. Today I am going to be in a chorus assembly, so I took a little more time than usual getting ready. I wanted to be sure that my hair looked nice, and I chose my favorite necklace (with a heart on a chain) and dangle earrings to wear. I get lots of compliments when I wear that jewelry.

Mom and Dad were in a good mood this morning, too. I helped fix breakfast, and we talked while we sat at the table. My little brother and sister are so cute and sweet. I really like it when we can start off the day with this family time. Mom said she liked my dress, and Dad even told me my smile was pretty. Boy, hearing things like that makes me feel so good I want to hug everyone I see!

When I got to school I joined my friends as usual. I can hardly wait to see everybody and catch up on the latest news. I have a lot of friends, and I feel good when I am with them. I want to spend as much time with them as I can, so this morning ritual is a great way to start my day. Most of the kids in our school have been together since elementary school, so I know almost everyone. Each year some new kids join the school, though, and it's nice to get to know them, too. For the most part I get along well with everyone, although I do have some friends who are closer than others. I spend as much time as I can with my special group of close friends. We get together after school, on weekends, and

as much as we can in school. In fact, sometimes I work my class sched-ule so I can be in the same classes with my best friends. We try to get our lockers close together so we can touch base throughout the day. We talk for hours on the telephone and chat together on the Internet when we're home. I'm usually the one who people come to when they have a problem. I genuinely want to help them by listening to them, being sensitive to their feelings, and empathizing with their situations, and they seem to appreciate my help.

My mom says sometimes I'm too compassionate for my own good. She thinks I'm too wrapped up in other people's problems. I am a pushover for lost and injured animals. Almost every month I find a stray cat or dog. I beg my parents to please let me keep them, but we always have to take them to the shelter. I feel terrible about leaving them there, but my dad says we wouldn't be able to walk through our house or backyard if I kept all the animals that I protect. He thinks sometimes I'm too warm-hearted.

I really do enjoy being around people, and most say I'm warm and friendly. It's really important to me that others like me, and I will go out of my way to please or help others if I can. My best friend, Julie, some-times tells me I'm too sweet and that people might take advantage of me, but that doesn't happen very often.

I have always liked school. I have particularly good memories of elementary school. Most of my teachers were so kind and caring. They really seemed to genuinely love kids. They took time to really get to know us and treated us kind of like we were all one family. The only teacher I had problems with was my fifth-grade teacher. Ms. Alegro seemed to like me at the beginning of the school year, but before the end of the year she began acting like she didn't like me at all. It seemed as if she criticized everything I did. I tried really hard to please her, but nothing worked. I felt so awful about it that I told my parents. My father suggested I talk to Ms. Alegro to see what was wrong, and finally I did. She told me she did not dislike me, but she never said she liked me. I spent the rest of the year trying to be good, and she seemed to try to be nicer, but the relationship never was right. I remember clearly how difficult it was to be in her class during that time. My grades that year were the worst they have ever been. I guess the support I got from my parents and friends was what helped me get through it. After all, I still have lots of wonderful memories of good times with people other than her.

The thing I liked most about middle school was getting to know so many new kids from other elementary schools. But having so many dif-ferent teachers each day was sometimes a challenge. Many of the teach-ers seemed to focus mostly on their subjects. They were not quite as personally involved with students as the teachers in elementary school. My favorite teacher was Mr. Fox, my English teacher. We read plays, poems, and short stories and discussed them in literature groups, where we shared our feelings and ideas about what we had read. We also met in small groups to share our writing assignments and get help with revi-sions and editing from the other kids or the teacher. I learn better when I can work with others instead of alone.

That's true even in high school. I am a good student, and I really do my best in classes where we are encouraged to participate in discus-sions and interact with the teacher and other students. I really enjoy classwide and schoolwide peer tutoring, where we give and get help from others. Working with a partner or in cooperative learning groups helps me learn. I don't care for classes where the teacher lectures most of the time and doesn't let students interact, and I have a really hard time when we have to give presentations or stand up in front of the class alone. I get so nervous, I often forget what I'm supposed to say or do.

Having a good relationship with my teacher is really an important part of learning for me. When my teachers let me know they care about me as a person, I work harder to meet their expectations. I need for them to approve of me, accept me, and recognize me. I do best in the classes where the teachers call students by their names, greet us at the door with a warm word or smile, and take the extra minute to chat with us about things we're interested in. When the teacher says something genuinely nice about me, I feel really good. In fact, that's more important to me than getting good grades or being told that I do good work. But I do whatever needs to be done to get good grades because the grade shows that the teacher is pleased with me, and my parents will be happy with my performance.

When I do have trouble learning something, it's usually because I'm worried that someone—either the teacher, a friend, or my parents—is not happy with me. When that happens, I have a hard time concentrating on what I'm supposed to be learning, or I get confused about what is important and make careless mistakes. For instance, last week I had a really hard time when my biology teacher scolded me in front of the class for whispering to my best friend, Julie. We were actually discussing part of the homework assignment, but the teacher didn't understand. She's pretty strict about talking in class and doesn't let us work together very often. She's one of those "learn from my lecture" teachers who seem to feel it's not important for students to interact with each other. That's really hard for me, but I try to please her by not socializing at all during her class. When she got mad at me, I felt so embarrassed and humiliated. I couldn't think straight for the rest of the class. I felt like crying when I got to the hall after class. Julie helped me feel better and pull myself together so I could get through the rest of the day. Now I'm especially nervous each time that I come into the science room. I have trouble paying attention because I'm concentrating so hard on not talking to anyone else.

Most of the time I really like school, and I do well in my classes. My other teachers seem to like me and show they appreciate having me in class. When this happens, I feel wonderful and I really do my best work.

CHARACTERISTICS OF REACTOR STUDENTS

Reactors are described by their friends and family as sensitive, kind, compassionate, and warm. They make up 30% of the population in North America. Out of this group, 75% of Reactors are female, and 25% are male (Kahler, 1974).

Reactors enjoy it when they can start the day by pampering their senses (Kahler, 2000). They immediately notice the weather, and they are highly sensitive to the moods of others. When everyone in the family is in a good mood and can sit down to breakfast as a family, for example, the Reactor can start the day happily. Wearing carefully chosen clothes, Reactors take special time selecting their accessories and appreciate being noticed for their good taste.

In order to do his or her best throughout the school day, the Reactor needs to connect with others. Meeting friends and exchanging the latest social news, listening to people's problems and dispensing advice, and getting counsel and support from friends about any problems of their own gives the Reactor a battery charge for the day. Periodically checking in with friends and being able to share feelings and reactions to the various aspects of the school day keeps the Reactor feeling good and able to concentrate on schoolwork.

Whether Reactors do well in class depends, for the most part, on their relationship with the teacher. If they feel that the teacher likes them and they are able to please the teacher, then Reactors will work hard to do well in the class. If they feel disliked or ignored, however, it is very difficult for them to concentrate on the subject matter, and they may spend a lot of mental energy thinking of ways to try to get the teacher to like them. If they are reprimanded, either in front of the class or privately, they are likely to become teary and even start to cry. They can be devastated when they feel they have let down someone they are trying to please.

Reactors enjoy school the most when they have opportunities to work with others. Their compassion for and desire to work with others can get them into trouble in class, however, because these needs often overshadow classroom requirements to listen or to work alone.

Cooperative learning groups, peer tutoring, and partner projects enable them to bounce their thoughts off others and to get validation for their ideas. This helps instill confidence in them so that their creative energies can flow. Teachers should be aware that Reactors are vulnerable to feelings of inadequacy. When this happens, they are easily flustered and can temporarily forget information and techniques that they have already mastered.

Table 2.1. Reactor (Feeler) needs: Personal attention, appreciation, sensory satisfaction

Help your Reactor students by
- Greeting them by name with a smile every day
- Complimenting them on their appearance
- Telling them how much you like their smiles
- Spending a few minutes talking with them every day
- Making a special "nest-like" place in the classroom where they will feel comfortable
- Having pets in the classroom
- Letting them keep a stuffed animal on their desk when taking a quiz or test
- Providing cookies or snacks for the class occasionally
- Telling them how much you appreciate having them in the class
- Allowing them to work in groups with their friends
- Encouraging them to discuss their feelings and ideas with other kids
- Providing opportunities for them to be peer tutors
- Involving them in cooperative learning group activities
- Allowing them to hold a stuffed animal or puppet when they have to give an oral presentation to the class
- Recognizing them as people as well as recognizing their work
- Allowing them to socialize during class occasionally
- Placing them in charge of caring for the class pet or plants
- Having live nature exhibits in the classroom
- Holding class outside on nice days
- Encouraging them to be peer buddies with new students
- Encouraging them to be peer buddies with students with disabilities
- Writing personal comments on papers to support grades

From Kahler, T. (1982). *Personality pattern inventory validation studies.* Little Rock, AR: Kahler Communications, Inc., and Kahler, T. (1996). *Personality pattern inventory.* Little Rock, AR: Kahler Communications, Inc.; adapted by permission.

Reactors will work for grades in order to please their teachers and their parents. They do their best when teachers show that they care about them and are happy with them. They appreciate when their papers and projects are selected for display. In fact, they have an "eye" for setting up displays and bulletin boards so that they are aesthetic and attractive.

Because they are able to be so empathetic, Reactors have a talent for making new friends and helping new students feel part of the class. They enjoy helping with all aspects of school life, from passing out papers and greeting new students to helping other students with their work. They also are good at organizing social events, such as a school or club party. They prefer to join clubs with their friends and like it best when any group of which they are a part functions as a close-knit family. Reactors need to feel appreciated and recognized just for being who they are. A sincere compliment or a greeting by name at the door when they arrive can set the tone for a positive day.

Reactors do their best when their presence is valued and when their personality traits are admired. (See Table 2.1 for more suggestions for supporting a Reactor.)

A TEACHER'S STORY

This story demonstrates miscommunication between a Persister teacher and a Reactor student in distress. As the teacher addresses the student's need for recognition of person, the student overcomes her self-doubt and responds more positively to the learning environment.

Maria is a student in my third-grade class who arrived in the United States 5 months ago from a country immersed in civil war. She always greets me with a smile and lights up when I smile back. She is warm, affectionate, and sweet. The other day another student, Karl, came back to school after being absent for 2 weeks. As soon as Maria saw Karl, she told him, "Oh, we're happy that you are back. We've missed you. Are you okay?" and she patted him on the shoulder.

Maria works well with any student with whom she is grouped. Math is her strongest subject, and often the other students ask her for help. She loves to help them, and she goes into her motherly role. Everything goes well except when she has to read out loud in class. When she is reading and has a hard time with a word or concept, she begins to make negative comments about herself. Then she slows down her rate of reading and participation. She needs constant reassurance to continue reading. If she gets too flustered, she starts to cry a little.

At first, I had many conversations with Maria about the importance of practice so she could learn to read fluently in English. I also told her that crying would not help the situation and she should not worry about making mistakes in front of the other students.

When I noticed that she was still engaging in these behaviors I decided to take a different approach. I told her to imagine a baby who can't walk and who—little by little, with practice—learns to walk. Learning to read in a second language is a process similar to that of a developing child. I reminded her that a similar process occurred when she learned to read in her native language. She could relate to this because she has several younger brothers and sisters. I now make a special effort to reassure her that it is okay to make mistakes, and I tell her frequently that we're happy that she is part of our class. I also remind her how grateful I am that she helps the other students in math. When I give her praise for being in our classroom and being helpful, she beams! The baby analogy seems to have helped her. When she has to read, she expresses more confidence and doesn't focus so much on her mistakes.

The Persister teacher is motivated by recognition for her work and her convictions. As the story points out, these were not effective with Maria. When the teacher realized Maria was a Reactor whose motivational need is recognition of person, she shifted to Maria's language and used an analogy that appealed to Maria's emotions: She related a story about a little baby learning to walk. The teacher reinforced this by giving Maria personal attention and telling her that everyone was happy she was in the class. She added that she appreciated her willingness to help other students in math.

Because the teacher is a Persister, she probably is giving the Workaholics and Persisters recognition for their work automatically. This recognition of Maria as a person is a nonmotivator for many of the other students in the class, but it is the driving force for Maria.

NURTURE AND CARE ABOUT OTHERS!

WILL WORKAHOLIC

THE THINKER

CHAPTER 3

A STUDENT'S STORY

I'm Will Workaholic. I usually get up early to look over my homework and class notes so I am prepared for the day. After I eat a good breakfast and fix myself a nutritious lunch, I arrive at the bus stop at precisely 7:30 A.M. The bus driver has been so unreliable lately—she comes anywhere from 7:30 to 7:40, which can really throw off my whole  schedule. At 7:55, if I'm lucky, I arrive at school and hit the library to meet my friends so we can double-check our homework with each other.

I arrive early for first period, which is English. Last semester I had the most disorganized English teacher—she took a long time to grade our papers, and I never knew where I stood in her class. Every time I asked her what my grade was, she would say, "Why do you want to know?" Can you imagine? Why wouldn't I want to know? I couldn't tolerate her irresponsibility any more, so this semester I transferred to a class with a teacher who is more reliable and organized, and I'm much more comfortable. He gave us a syllabus at the beginning of the semester that helps me organize my time better. He also provides us with rubrics for each assignment so I know exactly what I need to do to get an A, and I always know my exact percentage at any given time.

Second period is history, which is okay. The teacher is a very concerned person, who is always asking us how we feel about things. I wonder what that has to do with school and grades and my goals, but I just get the work done, and if there is time left over, I do my other homework in her class. I remember lots of my teachers from elementary school being like that—talking in soft voices (except when they got mad at someone!) and always trying to make the classroom comfortable and worrying about if we were all getting along with each other. Sometimes they would concentrate so much on those aspects, they would forget to put the schedule up on the board, which would upset my whole day. Their favorite teaching style seems to be those cooperative groups. I've always preferred to do my own work so that it's just the way I like it. When I'm part of a group, I tend to be in charge. I always seem to end up doing most of the work, especially when I get frustrated with the other members for goofing off or I'm afraid they won't get the work done on time. When I'm in charge of the group, I try to make the other members work hard so that they do the best job possible.

I'm the vice president of the sophomore class, so between second and third periods I have to dash down to the office to drop off the organizational chart I made of who is responsible for each event at Homecoming. I'll be going to both the game and the dance, mainly to make sure that everyone is doing what they are supposed to so that everything from the floats to the band are perfect and right on time!

Third/fourth period is one of my favorite classes—advanced placement (AP) biology. Generally, sophomores aren't allowed to take AP classes, but I asked if I could take a qualifying exam to get in. I don't think they actually had one, but someone made one up, and I passed it so I'm in. I have to study really hard in that class to keep up, but I'm into it. It is challenging, and my teacher is really smart. I respect her a lot. Right now we are preparing projects for a science fair. I'm going to enter, and I hope I win a prize or at least an honorable mention. I'm starting to put together my high school portfolio, and I want to make sure there are lots of academic awards included.

At lunch I like to go to the registrar's office where all the college materials are. I'm reading up on colleges so that I know where I want to apply. I've made a chart of the colleges I'm interested in, with accompanying columns of scholarships, expenses, and requirements. The college courses look so interesting to me! I'm going to see about taking more AP classes while I am in high school so I can take more advanced courses once I get to college.

During fifth period I have to take this course that all sophomores have to take—American government. It is so stupid! If you read the newspapers or any news magazines you already know how our government works. Most of this stuff I learned in eighth grade anyway. They don't have any AP government classes—they like those classes to be "heterogeneous." Some of the kids in that class are so lazy! They act very juvenile—all they do is talk about their boyfriends and girlfriends, and some of the dumbest ones fall out of their chairs on purpose and make sarcastic comments to the teacher. I feel sorry for the teacher having kids in the class who don't really want to learn. When I have sophomore class business or honor society stuff to take care of, I usually try to do it during that class. The teacher is pretty good about letting me out—he knows I can ace the course without even being there.

Sixth period is math. I find math really challenging and even fun sometimes. I like figuring out the formulas and seeing how the pieces all fit together. I took advanced math in middle school and last year, so I'm in a class with all juniors and seniors. I'm getting better grades than most of them. They don't seem to like me very much. I guess I show them up when I participate in class and get all A's on my quizzes and tests. They sometimes call me names because I'm the only one who has turned in all my homework so far in this grading period. I don't mind. I know what my goals are, and I'm on the path to reaching them.

After school I stay for football practice. I'm proud to be on this team even though it's only the junior varsity team. So far we are undefeated. We are really a good team, and I think the coach is going to appoint me

to be the co-captain of the team. I'll get to make up some of the plays and also help coach the team and call the plays.

I get home just in time for dinner. My parents and I usually talk about current events. I tell them what I did in school, and my parents tell me how their day was at work. Then I have to start immediately on my homework. Sometimes I have 4 or 5 hours of homework, but what else would I do in the evenings? Sometimes, if I don't have much homework, I relax and read *Newsweek,* but that's not very often. Lately some girls have been calling me in the evenings, but I can't talk long because it interferes with my homework. They usually want to talk about stupid things, such as who likes whom or how I feel about them. I can't be bothered with that kind of stuff. There is one girl in my history class I'm sort of interested in, though. I'm already making a list of what I can talk about with her if we go on a date. Maybe I'll call her for a study date.

CHARACTERISTICS OF WORKAHOLIC STUDENTS

Workaholics are by nature logical, responsible, and organized (Kahler, 2000). They make up 25% of the population in North America. Seventy-five percent of Workaholic students are male, and 25% are female (Kahler 1974).

Workaholics usually make very good students and cause their teachers little trouble. In fact, in her study on attention deficit disorder and personality type, Rebecca Bailey (1998) found that Workaholics were the least likely of all of the types to have attentional problems in the classroom. They are the students who can be depended on to complete their work on time and to do a good job. They usually know the schedule and prefer to organize their own time. Grades and recognition for their work are important to them. If a Workaholic student has a learning disability or developmental disability and is not experiencing academic success and recognition, school can be an extremely stressful place.

Workaholics, luckily, tend to have many personality traits in common with their teachers, especially with typical secondary school teachers. They take school seriously and see it as a means to a goal. Most Workaholics enjoy learning and go out of their way to take challenging and difficult courses to keep themselves stimulated.

Workaholics usually formulate their own organizational systems. They might use a notebook with dividers, color-coded pocket folders, handheld computers, and probably more than one calendar. They can multitask and respond to timesaving, efficient devices such as digital organizers and watches that have built-in calendars, alarms, and e-mail access. They enjoy hard work, especially if it pays off in some form of recognition for their accomplishments. They also like timed tests so they can get additional recognition for finishing

Table 3.1. Workaholic (Thinker) needs: Recognition of work and time structure

Help your Workaholic students by
- Displaying a daily schedule
- Providing a syllabus with due dates
- Acknowledging and rewarding accomplishments
- Providing a calendar for long-range projects
- Providing opportunities for them to make lists and cross off items as they are completed
- Encouraging them to take a class that adds a skill
- Returning graded assignments promptly
- Putting grades and comments on all work
- Displaying work on bulletin board
- Encouraging them to share their successes and accomplishments with you and their classmates
- Encouraging them to keep a journal
- Encouraging them to ask you or their friends for praise for their accomplishments
- Encouraging them to display certificates, plaques, or awards for their accomplishments
- Creating classroom awards
- Listening to and encouraging their ideas
- Letting them be the "helper" to explain or teach
- Encouraging them to mentor other students
- Encouraging them to create their own certificate for doing what is most important to them
- Having them do something around the classroom where they can see immediate improvement and get a reward
- Telling them, "You are good enough without being perfect." "You are entitled to be successful."

From Kahler, T. (1982). *Personality pattern inventory validation studies.* Little Rock, AR: Kahler Communications, Inc., and Kahler, T. (1996). *Personality pattern inventory.* Little Rock, AR: Kahler Communications, Inc.; adapted by permission.

quickly. Awards, plaques, recognition assemblies, good grades, certificates, and letters of recognition are soul food for the Workaholic. Even such comments as "good work," "great job on that paper," or "terrific ideas" can make the Workaholic's day.

Workaholics like routines—they get thrown off when the schedule changes. Their expectation is that classes, meetings, practices, and even meals will start on time. An agenda, syllabus, or class schedule will help a Workaholic's ability to predict the sequence of events and add to his or her comfort level.

Although Workaholics are stimulated by group discussions and debates, they prefer to produce their own work products. Too many times the Workaholic in the group project takes over, does the bulk of the work, and becomes agitated when others don't work up to his or her standards. They like to have tasks done well ahead of time. Workaholics prefer to deal in facts—concrete subjects such as math, science, history, and computer applications appeal to them.

Workaholics don't care for students who fool around in class and distract the learning situation. They become frustrated if they think that a class is a waste of their time and will often find other "work" to do (e.g., e-mail a friend, read a book, do their homework).

Often, Workaholics are called "bookish" names by their peers because of their dedication to hard work. Their idea of leisure might be to read a news magazine or a history or science book or to watch an educational television program. Possible ways to help Workaholics get their recognition of work and time structure needs met are included in Table 3.1.

A TEACHER'S STORY

This story demonstrates miscommunication between a Reactor teacher and a Workaholic student, Tranh, who is in distress. As the teacher changes the channel of communication and meets the Workaholic's need, she helps Tranh out of distress.

As Tranh entered my class the other day, I greeted him with my usual enthusiastic "Good morning!" He abruptly replied, "Will we be getting our tests back today, Ms. Johnson?" I replied that I couldn't give them back because some of the students had been absent and still needed to take the test. "Well, could we at least see our grades, then?" I reluctantly admitted that I hadn't quite finished grading and recording them because my cat had gotten sick yesterday and I had taken him to the vet. I promised him I would try to get them finished before the period was over. He huffed back to his seat. I reassured him by saying, "Dear, sweet Tranh, you are so conscientious and businesslike. I am sure you did just wonderfully on the test." His response was to glare at me.

Tranh is the best student in my advanced algebra class. He is logical, organized, and can apply what he learns to other situations. On this day, the students were going to be working in their study groups to solve 10 problems as a review before moving on to the next unit. I told them to divide the problems up however they wanted, but to make sure that everyone in the group knew how to do each type of problem.

As the students began working, I recorded the test grades. As usual, Tranh had done extremely well and had received the highest grade in the class. Just then, I heard a commotion at one of the tables. When I looked up, I saw that it was Tranh's group. I could hear him saying, "This is a stupid idea to have each of us do two problems. I am smarter than all of you and can do all 10 problems before anyone else can do their two. This is just a big waste of time for me." At that point, I interceded and took Tranh aside and said, "Honey, what's wrong?" He replied, "It would be a lot easier if we had our tests back so we could see how we did each type of problem. Besides, nobody in our group knew who was going to do which problems or how much time to spend on the assignment or when we were supposed to be finished."

At this point, I decided it would be a good idea to give Tranh some sort of recognition for the good work he does in my class. I told him I had finished grading the tests and that he had received the highest grade in the class. I told him what a good student he was and how the other students in the group would benefit from his expertise. I asked him to be the one to make sure that all the students in his group knew how to work every problem. I added that in 15 minutes I would assign their homework for tomorrow. Tranh returned to his group with a confident smile on his face and immediately got to work helping his group members with the problems.

People tend to try to motivate others the way they want to be motivated. In this instance, the teacher is a Reactor whose need is for recognition of person. Consequently, she tried to motivate Tranh by using the language of her favorite channel—the Nurturative channel. Calling him "Honey" and "dear, sweet Tranh" was her way of letting him know she cared about him as a person. However, Tranh was not open to the Nurturative channel and was not motivated by recognition of person. In fact, this type of comment grated on his nerves. As a result, he became distressed and glared at the teacher. As a Workaholic his motivation was to be recognized for his work. His act of bragging that he was smarter than the other students is a symptom that could let the teacher know that Tranh's need for recognition for work was not being met. When the teacher recognized this, shifted to Tranh's favorite channel, and gave him recognition for his work, his negative attitude toward the teacher and his bragging to the other students stopped. He became cooperative and began using his superior skills to help the other students rather than boasting about himself and putting them down.

THINK CLEARLY AND SOLVE PROBLEMS!

PAUL PERSISTER

SCHOOL COUNCIL

THE BELIEVER

CHAPTER 4

A STUDENT'S STORY

I am Paul Persister. I wake up in the morning when it is time to get up. I believe the
world is a serious place, and I take it very
seriously. In my opinion, Benjamin Franklin
was right when he said there will be plenty
of time in the grave to sleep. I believe everyone should have the opportunity to go to
school, so I look forward to the day. I believe
in taking care of my body so I wash, brush my teeth, get dressed, and
go downstairs to eat my breakfast. After breakfast I get my books and
materials ready and walk to school.

My mom makes breakfast for me and makes my lunch. I don't
always like what she makes for me, but I eat it because she made it,
and I believe we should not waste food. When I was in elementary
school she would pick my clothes out for me to wear. Now I am in high
school, I decide myself what I am going to wear. I eat a nourishing
breakfast at a leisurely pace because I always have plenty of time to get
to school. Sometimes my brothers and sisters slow me down a little
because they take too long in the bathroom. That's not the way it
should be, but I don't let it keep me from being on time for class.

When I was in elementary school, my teacher nominated me for
the school patrol, and I was selected, probably because I am reliable
and conscientious. I took my patrol duties seriously, and I was always
on time. If I say I will do something, I will do it. I stayed on patrol duty
until the bell rang, so I was always late to class, but it was an excused
tardiness.

Now that I am in high school, I am captain of the debate team. Debating is particularly interesting to me because we get to give our opinions, and we have to persuade the judges and the audience of the
correctness of our position. If I believe in something I tend to become
a leader in activities that revolve around it. For example, I believe that
we should help people who are less fortunate than we are. Therefore,
I suggested that we collect blankets and baby clothes for the families
in war-torn countries. My teacher agreed that this was a good project
and placed me in charge of it.

I don't have many friends because it takes time to trust someone enough to call that person a true friend. Most of the kids in my class are okay, but I'm not real close to any of them except Juan. I can trust him completely. We usually meet in the library before school and talk about things that interest us. I believe a few of the kids in my school are real jerks. Mostly these kids are bullies who pick on me. I tell them to stop, but many times they don't. When that happens, I ignore them. I don't seem to fit in with a lot of kids, but I don't mind it. I don't need to be part of a pack.

Most of my other acquaintances are people who are in my Boy Scout troop or in my horseback riding class. Horseback riding and scouting are my two favorite things to do. I value horseback riding because it is one to one, me and the horse. I am pushing the horse, and the horse is pushing back. It is a battle of wills to determine which one of us is the stronger willed. My riding instructor keeps challenging me by giving me strong-willed horses to ride. So far, I have had the determination to ride them well.

I am committed to scouting, too. When I was in elementary school I took great pride in wearing my Boy Scout uniform to school. I always made sure I had it ready the night before because I believe it is important to be prepared. I have had a lot of camping and hiking experience with my family and with the scouts. I have had so much experience in difficult situations that I believe nothing can happen that I can't handle. I believe in scouts and have worked my way up to being an Eagle Scout and a leader in my troop. I also am active in my church. I am an acolyte and teach Sunday school to the younger kids.

I stay pretty busy during the week going horseback riding or to scouts. Then I go home and do my homework. Sometimes I have to babysit for my little brother. When we play a board game together, he often tries to cheat. I have to keep explaining to him how important it is to follow the rules. Sometimes he gets angry and throws the board game at me. I would prefer he not do that, but I believe it is my responsibility as his older brother to teach him what is right.

I do quite well in school. My favorite classes are science, math, reading, and social studies. Foreign languages are harder for me. Some of my science teachers make the classes interesting by doing little demonstrations while they are explaining things about properties, molecules,

and so forth. Sometimes they surprise us by deliberately messing up the demonstration to show what can happen if we aren't careful. This type of presentation makes a deep impression on me because it shows the importance of following directions and doing things right. I believe that anything worth doing is worth doing well.

In elementary school we used to have a morning assignment that I believe was just to keep us busy while the teacher took attendance, collected milk money, and took a head count for lunch. It was always easy and I usually finished very fast, but I did not see the value in doing it. I would have preferred to work on our projects or do assignments that were more challenging.

I have a great respect for authority and rules. I believe rules are important so I usually follow them. I get upset when others don't. When I was in elementary school I used to explain the playground rules to the students who were not following them. This sometimes resulted in the other kids getting angry with me, but I didn't care. I believed then, and I believe today, that it is important that everyone understand and follow the rules. Sometimes the kids would tell me to stop "bugging" them, and sometimes they even told me that they did not like me. I didn't care because in my opinion it was more important that they respected me for standing up for what I believed in.

I usually am very quiet and rarely volunteer in class. My elementary and middle school teachers used to tell my parents that they were sure I knew the answers, but I seldom volunteered so they couldn't give me credit. My parents told me to volunteer more, and once in a while I did, but I never believed it was necessary for me to prove myself to my teachers. I knew that I understood the material, and that was good enough for me.

When I first enter a room or am placed in a new situation, I usually stand back and survey the situation until I understand what is going on and how I fit in. For example, when I get a new teacher I usually wait to see what he or she does when the other kids act out. Once I see how the teacher reacts to the situation, then I know how to act in that class.

I can work alone, with one partner, or in groups, but I prefer independent work so that I can do things my way. When I work alone I can do what I want, when I want. When I work with others, sometimes they end up using my work, slowing me down or studying things I already know.

I believe grades are important because they tell me something about myself. They assess my mastery of a subject as well as provide a way for me to measure my personal best. It is important for me to understand a subject so I can explain it to others who may be having difficulty. In addition, if I don't get good grades, my parents won't let me go horseback riding or participate in scouting activities. Another reason I want to get good grades this year is so that I can take courses next year that interest me. For example, if I don't get good grades this year, they won't let me take courses such as honors biology. These courses will help me when I get to college. If I have to study hard to get good grades, then I will. One of my strengths is my ability to stick to something until I get it done. I do that with my homework and with everything I am interested in.

CHARACTERISTICS OF PERSISTER STUDENTS

Persisters are dedicated, observant, and conscientious (Kahler, 2000). They filter the world through their well-established beliefs and opinions. Persisters make up 10% of the population in North America. Seventy-five percent of Persisters are male, and 25% are female (Kahler, 1974). Because they are able to follow routines well and usually are compliant, they present few problems in the classroom. Some of their strengths are their ability to stick with a project until it is completed, their inclination to ignore initial rejection of something they believe in, and their loyalty to their friends. Because their word is their bond, they become highly offended when someone questions their integrity. They are driven to excel and to help others achieve their full potential; therefore, they frequently become leaders in activities they believe in. They usually portray an image of strength and in most situations will not show weakness.

Persisters tend to dress neatly and will follow the dress code. Providing opportunities for them to have their beliefs and opinions recognized encourages them to participate and show what they know. They display an interest and do well in subjects in which they see value and relevance or can readily share their beliefs and opinions. They tend to get good grades in subjects they consider worthwhile.

Persisters want to do everything well, so they prefer it when expectations are made clear and they know the ground rules. Therefore, they are most comfortable when the rules and routines are very clear. Because they expect themselves and others to do their personal best at all times, they can become overly critical if things are not happening the way they "should."

When Persisters enter a room for the first time, they stand back and observe what is going on in an attempt to understand the ground rules and what is expected of them. After they understand how they fit into a situation, they will move into the room and join in. They do not cultivate a wide circle of friends, nor are they particularly social in class. They may have only one or two close friends in whom they can trust and confide. Usually these people will be those who share their interests and beliefs. With friendship comes commitment to support friends in need. Sometimes other students are "turned off" by Persisters' bossiness, their insistence on having their own way, and their rigid adherence to rules. Persisters work best alone or with one other person. Being part of a group is not important to them.

Students who are Persisters need to be respected for their convictions. Getting their work done because it is important or they see the value in it is the motivation they need to persevere. Although they appreciate recognition for a job well done, it is not critical that they hear it from others. They are able to pat themselves on the back because they know that they are doing something worthwhile. They do value receiving a certificate for community service or recogni-

Table 4.1. Persister (Believer) needs: Respect for beliefs and recognition for work

Help your Persister students by
- Respecting them
- Encouraging and rewarding honesty and integrity
- Asking for and listening to their opinions
- Believing what they tell you unless they make a misstatement
- Discussing politics and current events
- Involving the class in community service activities
- Encouraging them to write letters to the editor about important issues
- Encouraging them to get involved in student elections
- Encouraging them to mentor or tutor other students
- Inviting them to make a list of "My 10 Most Important Goals" that they can update annually
- Being an example to them
- Not expecting them to be perfect (e.g., focus on what they have accomplished, not on what was not done "perfectly")
- Assigning projects on human rights, the environment, or other important issues
- Encouraging them to be peer mediators
- Providing opportunities for classroom debate
- Encouraging them to share their rationale for their classroom responses
- Setting up a safe environment to discuss ethical issues
- Providing opportunities for self-evaluation

From Kahler, T. (1982). *Personality pattern inventory validation studies.* Little Rock, AR: Kahler Communications, Inc., and Kahler, T. (1996). *Personality pattern inventory.* Little Rock, AR: Kahler Communications, Inc.; adapted by permission.

tion for accomplishing a difficult feat, however. They believe that anything worth doing is worth doing well, and they strive for perfection. They are aware of what they could have done better and therefore tend to deflect praise.

Persisters also respond to a challenge. Therefore, they do well in subjects that provide them with opportunities to work hard for a cause they believe in. For instance, getting them involved in a debate or discussion about a service project, hobby, or cause they support may provide an entry into class participation. In these instances, they will stick with a project until it is completed.

These students are very aware of both implicit and explicit rules and will become frustrated with others who do not follow the established standards. Young children manifest this in "tattling" on their classmates or bossing them around. Older students may verbally find fault with others and tell them what to do, or they may talk about them behind their backs with others who share their strong sense of values. They can become upset when other students display behaviors that go against what they believe in. For instance, they are especially critical of bullies who pick on younger or weaker students.

Persisters respond well to routines and value responsible behavior. They appreciate admiration and respect from their peers and teachers. Providing consistent adherence to standards, selecting topics with a cause that interests them, praising them for their commitment, and valuing their opinions and beliefs promote classroom success for this type of student. Table 4.1 lists several possible ways to motivate Persisters.

A TEACHER'S STORY

This story demonstrates miscommunication between a Workaholic teacher and a Persister student in distress. As the teacher meets the needs of the Persister student, the student is able to emerge from his distress.

Jason is in my freshman biology class. He is a conscientious student who always does his homework, follows the directions on the lab assignments, and writes his answers in complete sentences. He takes pride in his work. On the first day of class he asked me if I would change his seat because his lab partner would not do the lab by the procedure.

On one occasion, the groups were working on developing a poster on "The Five Kingdoms of Life." Each group was assigned one of the kingdoms. They were to illustrate and label parts of an organism in their assigned kingdom, then to write a short paragraph and put them together to develop an attractive poster.

Twenty minutes into the project, Jason came to me and explained that one of the students in his group was not doing the project correctly. He and the other members were working hard and following the directions. He explained that he did not think it was fair to have this student in their group and that he and the others were afraid their grade would suffer because of this one student. I asked him what he thought I should do about it. He suggested that he and the other three students work together as a group and that this student be removed.

I reassured Jason that his grade would not be affected by the student who was doing the project incorrectly. I did explain that I could not exclude any student from the group; however, I would talk to the student who was not doing the project correctly to make sure he understood the assignment and expectations. I also suggested to Jason that he take responsibility for explaining anything the other student did not understand.

Jason returned to his group and continued working. I redirected the other student, and he also returned to the group better able to do the project correctly. Later, I noticed that Jason was working patiently with him.

Jason is a Persister in distress. He needs to be recognized for his work and for his convictions. Persisters take assignments seriously and get into distress when others do not. In this instance, Jason was in distress because the other student lacked seriousness. The teacher recognized this, gave Jason recognition for his work, and suggested he assume leadership for his group, thus using his convictions about hard work to motivate others.

STICK WITH YOUR BELIEFS AND VALUES!

DORIS DREAMER

THE IMAGINER

CHAPTER 5

A STUDENT'S STORY

I'm Doris Dreamer. I am reflective, imaginative, and calm. I almost always am tired and grouchy weekday mornings and have trouble getting up. After I get up I was my face, brush my teeth, get dressed, and go downstairs. I have unusual tastes for breakfast. If I eat cereal, I don't have it with milk. I usually fix myself soup or something that I find in the refrigerator, such as leftover vegetables or mashed potatoes.

School sometimes is a negative experience for me, and many days I don't want to go. I worry about how bad the day might be and wonder what I can do to disappear. Some days I get sick just thinking about having to go to school. In middle school I figured out how to induce the symptoms of asthma, and I would fake an asthma attack so I did not have to go to school. I figured out how many days I could be absent from school before it became a problem, and I missed every one of them. My mother thought I was always sick. Weekends are different. I get up early because I don't have to go to school. I can stay home and do things I want to do.

I think about things and conceptualize ideas that other kids don't even see. That makes people think that I am different, so my classmates sometimes make fun of me in school. I have a problem doing more than two things at a time because I don't prioritize well. My teachers sometimes think there is something wrong with me and refer me for special help. When I was in middle school I stayed at school 2 days a week for one-to-one tutoring to get help with my homework. I get the idea that some of my teachers think that I am dumb and will never amount to anything.

When I first get to school I go to my locker, get my stuff ready, go to my first-period class, and then just hang out there until the bell rings and class starts. If I have a book I might read it. Sometimes I might sit with a friend. Most of the time we don't talk about anything. We just sit there, walk around together, or hang out while we wait for the bell to ring. If we do talk it might be about what we are going to do or some events that are coming up.

My favorite classes changed over the years depending on how creative my teachers were and how much they encouraged my imagination. If the teachers had interesting classes that included a lot of class projects and if they were enthusiastic about their subjects, then I did well in that class. If they didn't, then I did not do well.

In elementary school I learned very early that I was different and I cried a lot. My mother reports that I cried in the first grade and the teacher said, "She'll grow out of it. I'm just going to ignore her." And I didn't do well on achievement tests, especially multiple-choice tests because there really was no right answer. My favorite subjects were art and science. In the fourth grade I liked English and writing. My teacher encouraged me to write biographies. I enjoyed writing so much that I asked to go to summer school to take a writing course. The teacher I had in the summer between the fourth and fifth grades encouraged us to do creative writing and wrote on my folder that my writing was very good.

The teacher I had the following summer did not let us do creative writing. She made us drill on constructing sentences. I used the same folder I had used the previous summer. When the teacher saw the comments the previous teacher had made, she scribbled them out and wrote in negative comments. Since then I haven't invested a lot of time writing for school.

In middle school my favorite subjects were art and reading. In art I can pick a color and do something imaginative with the color I choose. In reading class we get about half an hour to read. That is very relaxing. In other classes it is hard to be original. The teachers don't try to do things in a different way. I don't care for sports or physical activities. In science the teachers just kind of drone on and on, and it's not very interesting. They don't make learning very imaginative. In seventh-grade science I had an A the first marking period because it was biology. It was about systems and constructing understanding. The second marking period was a lot of memorizing and repetition and I couldn't get it, so I received a D on my report card. I have a hard time learning this way

unless teachers explain the thinking behind it. I have to be able to relate things I have to memorize to something I am familiar with, otherwise I can't learn them. It is hard for me to go into a mechanical mode
if I can't get behind the subject . . . or feel it . . . or touch it . . . or see it . . .
or taste it . . . so that it makes some sense. If I were teaching something
that had to be memorized I would teach it through movement so the
kids could feel and understand what is behind the material.

Math is very aggravating. Sometimes I don't understand it. The only
math course I have done well in is geometry. I could see all the figures
and the relationships. I could construct different designs. I could understand the concepts. I got an A in geometry. Algebra was terrible. I did
not understand it and did not do well in it. No one explained it in terms
I could understand. I did not take any more math after that.

History can be interesting sometimes if the teacher allows us to be
imaginative. Most of the time I don't see any need to study history. I
don't see how it is ever going to help me. I did enjoy eleventh-grade
history. My teacher asked us to write a paper comparing Benjamin
Franklin to someone else. My teacher wrote on my paper that my ideas
were very deep and perceptive. That was the first time since elementary school that any teacher acknowledged me positively. I have decided I will be a teacher after I graduate from college. I want people
who are different to have someone who will understand and acknowledge them.

Sometimes I write my papers as poems. If the teachers like my
imagination I get a good grade. If the teachers don't think I followed
the rules, I get a D or an F. There is no middle ground. The grade I get
depends on my teacher. Some teachers think I do weird things on my
papers. Most kids just do what they think the teacher wants them to do.
I don't always do that. I know when I am not doing what the teachers
want me to do, but there are times when I make a choice to disobey
them. It is not a random act. Sometimes my spirit and who I am has to
come out regardless of the consequences. I do well in those classes in
which the teachers allow me to be original and encourage me to use
my imagination.

When we have work to do in class, I prefer to work alone. When I
was in elementary school, I used to move my desk away from the other

kids so I could have my own private space. Most of my teachers kept forcing me to bring my desk back near the other kids. They worried that I would be lonely if I worked alone. I got the impression that they thought there was something wrong with me because I wanted to work by myself. Being surrounded by the other kids all the time suffocated me. I was so overwhelmed I couldn't even think. It was like I was being punished.

Now that I am in high school, I have learned to work with groups of people, but I still prefer to work alone. I can work with people I get along with. If I don't get along with them, I can't get any work done. When I work in a group, the other kids usually exclude me. Sometimes I think my ideas are not as high quality as theirs and I don't want to share them. When I do share my ideas, they don't want to listen to me. They say I am not really working.

I don't volunteer much in English class. The teacher probably thinks I'm stupid. But recently some of the kids have begun to realize that I have deep insights into understanding poetry. They have been coming to me for help. When they do, I help them. The irony is that when they present my ideas in class the teacher praises them for being so smart. When that happens I lose respect for the teacher. It also makes me think there is something really wrong with me.

I would like to get good grades, but grades are not as important to me as positive feedback. The feedback has to be meaningful too, not just "Good job." I do not study to get good grades. I study to learn things. Learning to me is a combination of understanding and creating. I am inspired by understanding new ideas or concepts. I might expand on one of these concepts to write a poem. I like to explore new ideas in art, too. Sometimes I create my own cartoons or art forms. I also enjoy designing and sewing clothes and designing greeting cards with poems on them. I like to create and be novel and innovative.

I am not a leader in school. I am a very quiet person, and I am not comfortable trying to lead things. Also, I am not very popular with the other students. I do not have many friends in my school. Some of the other kids in my class are okay, but I don't associate much with them. They don't talk to me all that much. Some of them are mean spirited and make fun of me or try to embarrass me. Most of the people I respect are older. You might say they have a mentor relationship with me. I spend a lot of time alone or with older people like my grandmother or a 65-year-old woman in our church. I admire her very much and spend a lot of time with her.

With most boys I think I am elusive. I am not comfortable with them. When a boy pursues me, I get scared and tend to run away . . . to go into myself. I don't date much, but I have a boyfriend now. When we go out we talk about literature, what our dreams are for our futures, and what we like and don't like. I don't make any effort to impress him. I am myself, and he is himself. And we just click. He and I are really kindred spirits.

When I am not with my boyfriend I walk home alone. I call my mother because she told me to telephone her, eat a snack, feed the cat, wash the dishes, and then go upstairs. I used to start my homework as soon as I got home from school. Now, I've learned to do something that will relieve the stress of the day when I come home, so I go to my room and read a book or write poetry and just let myself be. Sometimes I cook dinner because I find pleasure in cooking. I can be alone and creative. Then I start my homework. It's painful, but I do it. It takes me about 2 hours, and then after dinner I go over it with my father for another hour. I don't watch television, and I rarely surf the web. I think the Internet is kind of dull. I spend a lot of time alone.

My mom believes we all should eat dinner together, so we eat together every night. My mom and I don't have much in common, and we don't communicate very well. She likes to talk about shopping and makeup, and I have no interest in those things. It's easier for me to talk with my dad. My father and I talk about history and novels. We also talk about intellectual ideas. He tells me to let him know what I am thinking. He enjoys it when I show him my art or read my poems to him. I understand my homework better when my dad uses real-life examples to explain it.

In school I think teachers could be more effective teaching me if they would use real-life examples or examples from movies or TV shows to illustrate the points they are making. Or they might use cartoons that show people what they are trying to say. In math they could make word problems out of cartoons. Then we could see what was happening and understand what the problem is. They could do the same thing in other classes, too. When they assign things I already know how to do, they can explain the lesson, tell me what they want me to do, and leave me alone to do it.

CHARACTERISTICS OF DREAMER STUDENTS

Dreamers are very interesting people and pose a definite challenge to teachers, many of whom do not understand how Dreamers perceive the world. Dreamers usually are very introspective and shy and have an entirely different outlook on the world around them than other people do. They are reflective, imaginative, and calm and are able to do repetitive jobs that other people might find dull, boring, or uninteresting (Kahler, 2000). They also make good writers because of their insights into themselves and other people. Dreamers make up 10% of the population in North America. Sixty percent of this group is female, and 40% is male (Kahler, 1974). Although they almost never get identified as having attention-deficit disorder with hyperactivity, a significant number of them get labeled as having attention-deficit disorder, inattentive type (Bailey, 1998).

The primary psychological need of Dreamers is for solitude. They need their own private time and their own private space every day. If they are forced to interact with other people all day, they tend to get into distress because they feel smothered. When this happens they are not able to think clearly and tend to withdraw into depression.

Dreamers may find it difficult to get alone time in elementary school because of the difference in personality type between them and their teachers. Most elementary school teachers are Reactors who need frequent contact and close association with other people and are not happy when they are alone for long periods of time. Therefore, they may become concerned when they see Dreamer students trying to move away from other students. When this happens, Reactor teachers may feel that Dreamer students are unhappy and may try to force them to become part of the group. Alternatively, they may ask other students, especially Reactor students, to include the Dreamer students in their activities. The end result of this intervention is that the Dreamers feel smothered and try to keep their Reactor classmates at arms length, causing the classmates and perhaps the Reactor teachers as well to feel rejected.

When Dreamers are in distress, they become unable to process information clearly, and they shut down. They withdraw into themselves and try to disappear into their imaginations. They build walls around themselves to keep others out. In extreme situations they may lock themselves in a closet to be alone or demonstrate some other behavior that others may perceive as bizarre.

In addition, Dreamers have difficulty when given more than two things to do. For example, if they have homework assignments in each of six classes, they may have difficulty prioritizing them. They may not be able to get started on any of them, or they may start all six, but not complete any. Teachers can help them by asking a parent, tutor, or another student to help them prioritize their assignments each day. Although most students do not like to be told what to do, it is essential to tell Dreamers precisely what is expected of them in an imperative, concise manner. Once Dreamers understand what to do, teachers should allow them some time to work alone.

Dreamers have an ability to look at things in ways that are very different from the ways others see things. They also conceptualize ideas in unique ways. For example, Einstein was most likely a Dreamer. The theory of relativity came from his ability to conceptualize the universe in ways that were different than those of any-

Table 5.1. Dreamer (Imaginer) needs: Direction and solitude

Help your Dreamer students by
• Giving clear directions for assignments
• Allowing them their own private space and some alone time
• Going to and initiating conversation with them, without expecting lots of feeling or long talk
• Encouraging them to be imaginative
• Helping them prioritize assignments
• Not insisting that they play a group game at recess
• Breaking down assignments—giving only one or two parts of the assignment at a time
• Seating them out of high-traffic areas
• Checking occasionally to make sure work is being completed and turned in
• Working with them each day to set priorities and focus on doing what is most important
• Helping them make lists and cross items off as they complete them
• Giving them written daily directions on the homework assignment

From Kahler, T. (1982). *Personality pattern inventory validation studies.* Little Rock, AR: Kahler Communications, Inc., and Kahler, T. (1996). *Personality pattern inventory.* Little Rock, AR: Kahler Communications, Inc.; adapted by permission.

one else. Yet, Einstein was expelled from school because he was so different. Michelangelo was a Dreamer. He looked at the Sistine Chapel ceiling and saw *The Creation* there. He painstakingly painted it while lying on his back for 7 years, meticulously painting each detail. The story is frequently told of Michelangelo seeing a block of granite, which had been discarded by another sculptor because he did not "see" anything in the stone. Michelangelo "saw" a figure in the stone, took it to his studio, and sculpted *The Pieta.* Thoreau was another famous Dreamer, in all likelihood. Thoreau went off to live by himself at a tranquil pond for 2 years and described his experience in his book *Walden,* a Dreamer environment.

For teachers, respecting the need of Dreamers to have alone time and their own private space is essential. The challenge for educators is to recognize the strengths of Dreamers, encourage their imagination, acknowledge them as people, and recognize their unique contributions. (See Table 5.1 for more ideas on teaching the Dreamer.)

A TEACHER'S STORY

This story demonstrates miscommunication between a Rebel teacher and a Dreamer student who is in distress. Understanding and meeting the needs of the student helped both the teacher and student reduce their distress levels in the classroom.

I was excited about the lesson I was preparing to do in one of my favorite classes! We had just finished the unit on explorers, and we were going to play a review game much like Jeopardy!, except instead of "buzzing" when they wanted to answer, the students were to throw a miniature basketball into a basket. The kids in this class are always energized, on task, and genuinely interested in history. Everyone, that is, except Alana. She never seems to get excited about anything. Sometimes she flashes me a quick smile, but that is about all.

Alana is a reflective, calm, and shy student in my sixth-grade class. I've been worried about her since the beginning of the year. I've even spoken with her parents about her lack of close friendships in the class and given them suggestions of how to get her to interact with other kids, such as having them host parties at her house. Whenever we do group work in the class, she works on the assignment by herself.

One other thing I would like Alana to do more of is participate in class. I call on her every day and even try to draw her out by joking with her, but she is so passive. She won't even tell me she doesn't know the answer. Most of the time she just looks at me with a helpless look on her face. Her parents reported that even when relatives come over, she often retreats to her room. They have explained that this is rude; however, Alana seems to prefer to be alone. They were considering counseling for her because they thought she was depressed.

On game day, I assigned each of the students to teams who met on different sides of the room. Alana took that opportunity to get a seat far in the back of the room by herself. I began to explain the rules of the game—make a basket, pick a category, hear the question, answer as a team (within 25 seconds or the other team may steal), hurry!

After a while, I noticed that Alana had pulled her desk even farther back and was sitting quietly. She looked miserable. I told the class to take some practice shots and went back to talk with her. After much prodding to find out what was wrong, she finally told me that she didn't want to play the game. I then said, "Alana, you must participate in the game; that is the lesson I planned for the day. You will be the score keeper." Alana reluctantly got up and joined the class. As she recorded the points for each team, I noticed that she was flashing me those little smiles of hers.

Recently, it occurred to me that Alana is nothing like me and maybe that's why she frustrates me so much. She truly doesn't seem to need a lot of people around her to be happy. She seems content and actually works the hardest when I make sure she understands the assignment and then leave her alone to do it. As long as I check back with her every once in a while and remind her to put it in the "finished box" when she is done, she completes her written work. Some of it is quite insightful.

I have noticed that recently she has made one friend in the class, so I have her sitting close to her new friend. Sometimes I use the technique of "think–pair–share": When I ask a question, I give the students time to think about the answer, talk it over with another person, and then share in the large group. I notice that Alana is more likely to know the answer when I call on her in those situations. I also tried another technique that worked pretty well. I told Alana in advance that during a certain part of the period (for instance, during our discussion on the 13 colonies) I was going to ask her a question about something specific. This also helped her participate better and now those little smiles of hers are more frequent!

Changes have begun to occur at home as well. Her parents have begun helping Alana get her need for solitude met. As soon as she gets home from school she is allowed to go to her room, shut the door, and relax by herself. Sometimes she reads a book or writes a poem or essay. Other times she just sits. After an hour or 2 she comes down to help make dinner. Many evenings she talks willingly with her parents at dinner before returning to her room. Recently, her parents reported to me that the last time relatives came over, Alana actually initiated conversation and asked if she could go to her room after dinner. Her parents said that as long as she came down to say good-bye when the guests left, that would be okay. Instead of resisting, Alana graciously came down and said her good-byes.

Although her parents and I are still worried about the amount of time that Alana likes to spend alone, her friendship in the classroom and her improved ability to complete her work are helping her grades to improve. Sometimes I still have to call her back from "dreamland," but I find that if I give her a direct command, almost like an order (which is a very uncomfortable way for me to interact!), she is more responsive.

As a Dreamer, Alana wants and needs her own private time and her own private space. Dreamers do not do well in an environment with a lot of noise and confusion. Alana's Rebel teacher likes to have people around and is energized by enthusiasm, action, fun activities, and by a number of things going on simultaneously. With these different needs, it is predictable that Alana might be in considerable distress in this teacher's classroom. In addition, Alana's parents are gregarious and frequently entertain at home. They have a hard time understanding how anyone can be happy when they are alone for long periods of time. As her teacher and her parents spoke to her in the Directive channel and allowed her to get her solitude needs met in school and at home, her grades improved and she became more willing to participate.

BE IMAGINATIVE AND REFLECTIVE!

RITA REBEL

THE FUNSTER

CHAPTER 6

A STUDENT'S STORY

Hi! I'm Rita Rebel. I'd love to tell you a little about what my day is like. I love to sleep in. I hate to get up in the morning, so I procrastinate to the last second and get up as late as I possibly can. I would sleep until noon or later if I could. When I do get up, I'm slow to get moving. Then I work frantically to get things done. I have convinced  myself that I am more creative and work best when I am under an intense time crunch and under pressure to produce. I do not have any set routine. I wash up and get dressed. I take my time. I go from *grumpy* to *happy.* By the time I go to school I'm in a good mood, and I look forward to whatever new things I can do that day. I know I am going to see my friends, find some new things to do, and have fun. Life can be a real high.

I don't plan what I am going to take to school, so I never get my things ready the night before. I wait until the last second and then run frantically around looking for my books and papers. Usually I manage to find everything, but sometimes I forget things or I can't find them. If I forget something, that's too bad, but it's no big deal. Frequently, I am late for my school bus, and my parents have to take me to the bus stop or all the way to school. Sometimes I am late for school, but I don't mind. I don't react well to schedules, and I don't like to plan my day or any activities. I like to take things as they come and play it by ear. I prefer to be spontaneous.

I am not a breakfast person. I usually don't eat breakfast unless my mom makes me eat something. When I was younger she used to make me have a glass of Ovaltine and milk with an egg mixed up in it. Sometimes all the egg would not get mixed up and there would be a piece of egg at the bottom of the glass, which would get stuck in my throat. YUCK!!! Most days though, I don't eat anything. If I am really hungry I might grab a Pop Tart as I run out the door. It really bugs me when people insist that I eat breakfast or force me to eat. Being forced into a routine bugs me. So do checklists. Mornings can be stressful if I haven't done my homework the night before because I have to squeeze it in somewhere.

When I first get to school I hang out with my friends. I am a social butterfly and I say, "Hi!" to everyone. I usually am the last one to get to my locker to get things because I wait until the last minute so I can talk longer with my friends. As a result I sometimes am late to my first class. If I am on time I am one of the last ones through the door.

I like the social aspects of school, but I don't like most of my classes. They are so boring and I don't do well in boring classes. I don't do well with ideas and theories either. I need concrete stuff that I can see. There are some exceptions, though. I love my physics teacher. She is the hardest teacher I have, but she makes physics fun. I built a rocket, went out to a field to launch it, and measured the acceleration. I built a bridge and tested it to destruction to see how much weight it would hold. I built a robot with flashing LEDs. I burned my hand using a soldering iron building the robot, but I didn't care because I had fun making it. That class is awesome. We had a substitute like that in chemistry class, too. She had us do a lot of cool things in the lab. One time we bounced around the room while we acted out solids, liquids, and gases. This teacher was great, and chemistry became my favorite subject that year.

How I feel about a course does not depend on how hard or how easy the course is, or even what the subject matter of the class is, except maybe when it's music or art. My reaction to classes is entirely based on the teacher. My seventh-grade math teacher was boring. All he did was teach from the book. We never had any fun, and I hated to go to his class. I also hated my algebra class. Algebra made no sense to me. X and Y are not numbers, so I had a hard time grasping what algebra was all about. But I loved my seventh-grade English class because the teacher made everything fun. Poetry usually is boring, but she made it come alive. I hate to diagram sentences, but she even made that fun. My eighth-grade English teacher was awful. All she did was stick to the textbook. Her class was right after lunch, and I used to sleep through her entire class. I hated her class. My high school English teachers have us role-play when we read plays, though. That is cool. I love role-playing, and the more we role-play in my classes the more I like the

class. My eighth-grade math teacher was awesome. She made everything interesting and fun. I loved going to her class. I even enjoyed doing word problems.

I like to work with groups of good friends. We can get a lot of creative stuff going. We fool around a lot, party, and have fun, but we get
our work done. In a group, I want to be the hub with my hands on
everything so that everything revolves around me. I don't like to work
in groups with people I don't like. I have a hard time getting any work
done. In fact, I may shut down if I have to work with people I don't like.

I've heard my mom's friends refer to me as a tomboy. I guess that's
because I play sports and love doing mechanical things. My dad is a
mechanic, and I help him in the shop a lot. I use an acetylene torch to
make faces out of light bulbs. That is fun. I am very creative, and I like
classes that let me use my creativity. Unfortunately, not too many of my
teachers encourage me to be creative.

I am a student leader. I am in a lot of extracurricular activities. I love
to sing and act. I have the lead in the spring musical. I love to be cen-

ter stage. I am a soloist in the chorus, and I am captain of the Science of the Mind Spontaneous Team. I am treasurer of my class and a national officer in my high school sorority. I love the closeness of being with fun people, and I like to laugh with my friends. I am pretty popular in school because I amuse people. As a result, a lot of kids want to hang out with me and have fun with me. I probably have at least as many friends who are boys as friends who are girls. Most of my close friends are like me.

I tend to prefer to do my homework by myself. If I understand the subject matter, I want to do the work when *I* want to do it without anyone pressuring me to get it done. I hate to rewrite things or proofread something to make sure I have spelled everything correctly. There is no fun in that, so I don't do it. If I don't understand something I probably won't do the assignment anyhow.

I don't really care about grades. I can get good grades if I like a teacher, and I will work very hard in classes I like. Creativity is the hook to get me to produce. If I can express my ingenious talents in a class, then I will study hard. If I can't be creative, then school is a drag and I don't care if I get good grades or not. My parents are always giving me a pat on the back when I do well, and that is encouraging, too. That's not enough if the class is boring, though. I can't even think if the teacher does not use some ingenuity in class. I received a poor grade in my seventh-grade math class. It was like my brains were going to seep right out of my head. I get turned on by originality, innovation, and being able to play an active role. I need to have fun in order to have energy to work.

I love my computer class. Computers are fun. I really like the Internet because I can go anywhere and find out about anything I want. I can also meet any kind of person I want. I can do really fun things on a computer like designing creative programs and taking boring web pages and bringing them to life. I also love to play computer games.

It is better for me to have a boring class in the morning because I have more energy then. I have an energy drain in the early afternoon so I like to have my gym class right after lunch. That way, I can get re-energized. I like to hang out with my friends at lunchtime. I never make my own lunch before I leave for school, so I buy it in the cafeteria. I usually get french fries and ice cream. If my mom makes my lunch, I will eat what I like in it and throw the rest away. In elementary school, my mom gave me milk money every day, but I never bought milk with it. Instead I bought an ice cream sandwich.

I have a problem sitting in a confined seat for an hour. I am constantly shifting from side to side. I push my socks down, fidget, tap my fingers on the desk, and doodle. I have to get up from time to time. I have to be able to move around occasionally and make contact with other kids in my class. My teachers don't understand this, so I get in trouble sometimes and get placed in detention. When I get bored I will do something drastic to end the boredom. I might drop a book on the floor, fall out of my seat, pull the hair of the student in front of me, make a remark that makes everyone laugh, shout at the teacher or one of my classmates, or clown around. If the teacher gets mad and yells at me I may swear at the teacher, tip over a desk, throw a chair, or fight with a classmate. If I am using my creativity positively and am interested in a subject, then none of this happens and I usually can stay engaged for the entire class period.

I really like extracurricular activities. I spend tons of time on them. Although I like participating in sports, I hate spectator sports. I love acting in plays, singing in musicals, playing in the band, painting sets for the plays, and competing in the Science of the Mind Spontaneous Team. I have at least one extracurricular activity each term and usually more than one. I constantly get involved in more than I can do, and then I spend my time juggling my schedule to fit everything in. I always overcommit to things and then I shut down. When that happens, I go AWOL and don't show up for activities.

I get home about 5:00 P.M. I may hang out with friends, put on some wild music, and sing and dance. I might also ride my bike, turn the television on loud, let my imagination run wild, and pretend I'm someone different, or go to the mall with my friends. I put off doing my homework as long as possible. Frequently, I don't do it until early the next morning. When I do my homework I have to have the TV or radio on. I work better when there is noise in the background.

I have a lot of male friends at school. Boys are more fun than girls are because they do more active and fun things. I like most people. I especially like high energy, fun people. I do not like quiet people. It isn't so much that I don't like them as it is that I don't have anything in common with them. I also don't like kids who act snobby or think they are better or smarter than everyone else is.

I like boys, and sometimes I go out on a date. When I date, I usually double date or go with a group. My goal is to have fun, so I like to go with more people because the conversation rarely lags in a group. Also there is less chance there will be any down time. When we go out I don't try to impress my date. I do my own thing. My attitude is "I am me." Take me or leave me the way I am. If you don't like me the way I am, too bad. My favorite topic to talk about on a date is me!

CHARACTERISTICS OF REBEL STUDENTS

Rebels are creative, spontaneous, and playful people. They react to everything that happens in their environment either positively or negatively. They have strong reactions to things and can switch from loving something to hating something in a microsecond. They usually are artistic in some way, have an excellent sense of humor, and are the most creative of all the personality types. Although Rebels make up only 20% of the population in North America (Kahler, 1974), they make up 55% of those who are described as most difficult to teach by educators, 65% of students who are labeled as having ADHD, hyperactive impulsive type, and 52% of students who are labeled ADHD, inattentive type (Bailey, 1998). In North America, 60% of Rebels are female, and 40% are male.

Although Rebels like to be with groups of people, they basically are loners who don't form close attachments to many people (Kahler, 2000). They have many acquaintances but not many close friends. They are individualists who are determined to do their own thing regardless of what anyone thinks of them. They dress to suit themselves—frequently outlandishly, and may dye their hair purple, have body piercings, or sport large or provocative tattoos. They can't stand being ordered around and hate it when people impose deadlines, structure, rules, and regimentation.

Many Rebels are kinesthetic learners. They like active, hands-on classes that give them a chance to use their creativity. They have a hard time sitting still for long periods of time unless they are actively involved in projects that interest them. Fun is their currency and is the criteria they use to measure the usefulness of any class. If a teacher stimulates them and they are having fun in a class, they will work very hard. If they are bored in a class, they will have no interest in the subject or project and will be unable to accomplish anything. Rebels do not like rules, regimentation, routines, or boring work. They hate most homework assignments because they view them as repetitive and boring. Homework assignments that allow them to use their creativity catch their attention, however, and they will work very hard to complete them.

Rebels can be a very positive influence in a class if they are motivated according to their needs. They are often the most creative students in the class and have wonderful senses of humor. Moreover, it is easy to keep them interested and stimulated if the teacher jokes with them or encourages them to get in front of the class to tell a joke, sing a song, recite a poem, act out a role in a play, or give a report to the class. However, Rebels are not motivated by A's and are not intimidated by consequences. They cannot be forced to do anything they do not want to do. They may react violently to shouting, threats, or being ordered around. (See Table 6.1 for more suggestions for helping Rebels to get their needs met.)

When Rebels get bored in class, they either tune out and use their imaginations to fantasize themselves in another environment or do something dramatic to change the environment they are in. They may find excuses to get up or move around. If they are challenged they may become stubborn or belligerent and may mumble under their breath or "talk back" to the teacher. If a situation becomes too unbearable for them, they may do something to get negative attention by swearing at their teachers, throwing chairs, tipping over their desks, hitting or kicking their classmates, and hitting or kicking their teachers. These negative behaviors that give Rebels a bad reputation and get them in trouble frequently will be greatly reduced or even disappear if the teacher will encourage their creativity and let them have some fun from time to time (Bradley & Smith, 1999; Jackson & Pauley, 1999; see Chapter 9).

Teaching Rebels can be challenging for a teacher. It also can be fun and very rewarding to encourage their creativity, to see how much they learn, and to watch them mature and grow.

Table 6.1.   Rebel (Funster) needs: Playful contact, fun

Help your Rebel students by

- Displaying a good sense of humor and being playful
- Letting them decorate the classroom with wild posters, lights, colors, or gadgets
- Encouraging them to play a sport, collect fun things, or play a musical instrument
- Going on field trips to interesting and fun places
- Providing an opportunity for them to get out of their seats and periodically move about in class
- Providing opportunities for them to present a report to the class
- Encouraging them to write a song or poem about a subject and to sing or read it to the class
- Encouraging them to be innovative and creative
- Providing opportunities to dress up to demonstrate educational concepts
- Providing opportunities for them to role-play during class
- Telling them a joke a day or letting them tell a joke to the class
- Encouraging them to create a skit or play to perform for the class
- Encouraging them to write a short story
- Encouraging them to write an article about the lesson
- Encouraging them to draw pictures illustrating the lesson
- Bringing in clever cartoons and sharing them with the class
- Encouraging them to bring in cartoons related to the subject
- Providing lots of multisensory experiences in each subject
- Encouraging group participation in games that teach or reinforce the lessons
- Encouraging them to do hands-on experiments in science
- Teaching in concrete terms; tying lessons to real-life experiences
- Doing the unexpected occasionally and varying voice intonation
- Giving them an opportunity to socialize occasionally during class

From Kahler, T. (1982). *Personality pattern inventory validation studies.* Little Rock, AR: Kahler Communications, Inc., and Kahler, T. (1996). *Personality pattern inventory.* Little Rock, AR: Kahler Communications, Inc.; adapted by permission.

A TEACHER'S STORY

This story demonstrates miscommunication between a Persister teacher and a Rebel student in distress. As the teacher helps the student get his need for playful contact met, the student is able to channel his energy and control his annoying behavior so that the student can fully partic-ipate in class activities.

It was Thursday and time for me to pick up my fifth-grade physical edu-cation class. My stomach clutched as I walked toward the classroom. As much as I like these students as individuals, together they are a chal-lenge when it comes to gym class. This is especially true of one of my students, Sam. I immediately spotted Sam on his way into line. He stopped halfway and sat on Sara's lap. Then he jumped up and nudged Jack before he spied me at the door. He lunged toward the door yelling, "All right, it's time for P.E.!" As the students lined up, I reminded them to be courteous to the other students working in their classrooms as we walked down the hall. Before my first word was out, Sam came bursting through the doorway, tripping over his own feet and pushing Lucy into the wall. "Oh, sorry Luce, but Jack pushed me." (In fact, Jack had not even come through the door.)

With the class finally on its way, I stuck close to Sam, and within seconds he was talking loudly to the person in front of him. I reminded him of the rules, and he mumbled, "I guess I didn't hear you." I could see it was going to be a long walk down the hall unless I changed my tactics! I pulled Sam aside and in my most enthusiastic voice said, "Hey, Sam! I've always wanted to know how many steps it is from your class-room to the gym. How about if you count them for me? This has to be our little secret because I'm going to have the other students guess, so don't let anyone else know what we're doing!" At last, Sam made it quietly down to the gym and whispered a number to me.

As we went inside, I was well aware of the temptations that awaited Sam, but I had to leave the equipment out. I hoped to get inside quickly enough to divert his attention until I could get him into his squad. "Once we do our stretching and a short relay, we'll get into our game for the day." I told him. "Are we playing dodge ball today?" yelled Sam. With a wink I told him, "I'm keeping the main event a surprise until after our warm-ups!" Warms-ups do not interest Sam, who immediately edged close to the balls that were stationed around the room. Sensing what Sam was about to do, I asked him to come up and lead the last stretch. As Sam waited for his turn in the relay, he hopped around and bounced himself off the mat on the wall. Finally, screaming as loudly as he could, he took off for the other side of the gym. As Sam ran with his arms flailing, he drew everyone's attention as he slid across the line. A few shouted comments and several chuckled. Sam entertained his audience!

As the students picked up the tennis balls they used in the relay, Sam "helped" by throwing tennis balls to the other end of the gym. "Hey, Sam, how about if you take this bag and jog to the other end of the gym and see if you can collect all the balls in 3 minutes flat! Go!"

"Okay, now the main event—we will play dodge ball for the rest of the class!" This drew moans from some of the girls and cheers from some of the boys. After a quick review of the safety rules, the game began. This was right up Sam's alley—running, throwing balls at people, and dodging the ball himself. Unfortunately, a scuffle between Sam and Jack over a ball went from friendly to serious. Sam's usually smiling face was masked with anger. As he made one last grab for the ball, he shoved Jack into one of the doors. At this point I had to blow the whistle and stop the game. I yelled at both of them to sit on the bench.

As the rest of the group resumed the game, I went over to talk with Sam and Jack. "What was that all about?" I asked. Immediately, Sam jumped in with "It's Jack's fault. . . . " "No, it's *both* of your faults, and I want you to be more careful in the future. I want you to sit on this bench and cool off!" Then I remembered Sam's need for fun and action so I added, "Sam, you watch who gets hit with the ball and see how long it takes for everyone to get out." I made sure that Sam was able to rejoin the game after a few minutes of time out.

As the students finally lined up to leave, Sam and Jack were friends again and acted as if nothing had happened. I realized that Sam was wound up again and still needed to make it back to class. I told Sam I was going to watch him walk down the hall, and at each classroom door

I wanted him to turn around and look at me to exchange a "secret signal." I noticed that he was able to make it to his classroom without incident!

Rebels need playful contact. If they get it, they can channel their creativity and spontaneity in a positive direction. If they do not get it, they often engage in negative behaviors so rebellious that they are given detention, sent to the principal's office, or expelled from school. Miscommunication between a Persister teacher and a Rebel student is very likely. Sam's Persister teacher could very easily have sent Sam to the principal's office for his behavior, but she did not. Instead, she made walking down the hall and having a prominent role in the class activity fun. As a result, Sam stopped his disruptive behavior and stayed on task. Because the teacher's Rebel personality part was not well developed in her structure, it took a lot of energy for her to deal with Sam in a successful way. As she continues to develop and strengthen the Rebel part of her own personality, meeting Sam's needs will become easier.

PLAY, HAVE FUN, AND BE CREATIVE!

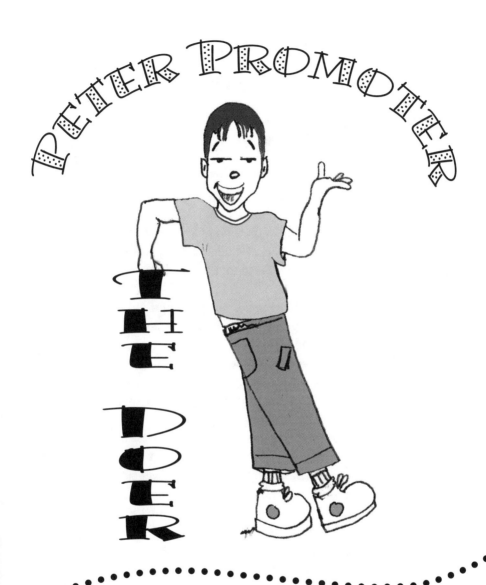

PETER PROMOTER

THE DOER

CHAPTER 7

A STUDENT'S STORY

Let me introduce myself. I'm Peter Promoter. I usually start the day with a bang. I jump out of bed with an attitude of "Good morning world! What exciting things are going to happen today?"

After I get up, I brush my teeth and wash up. I set the fashion for the school, so I have to look good for "my people." I know I am going to use a lot of physical energy all day, so I eat a big breakfast of eggs, ham, toast or bagels, coffee, and juice. When I was in elementary school I used to drink milk and juice, but now I drink coffee. I started drinking coffee when I was 12.

I look on school as a challenge. Challenges turn me on, so I buzz around, getting my stuff together so I can grab everything at the last minute as I head out the door to go to school. I'm on top of the world.

I have to get some physical exercise, so I have energy to get through the day. When I was in elementary school I would go out to the playground and play on the equipment or play games as soon as I got to school. Now that I am in high school, I stop at the driving range and hit some balls on the way to school. That's how I hone my skills in my best athletic event. I am the captain of the golf team and the best golfer on the team. I have been the best golfer on the team ever since my freshman year. I have entered several local tournaments, and I have won more than half of them. Also, morning is a good time for me to socialize, so after I get to school I hang out with my "buds." We look at things we can do in school and after school that will be exciting. My circle of friends has expanded each year because I have an ability to make friends with just about anyone. Hey, my classmates voted me "Mr. Confidence."

I was lucky in arranging my schedule because I have gym class second period. Having it then gives me a chance to get some physical exercise early in the day. That charges me up for the rest of the day. I am also hooked on speech; drama; and the action, danger, and excitement of military history, especially if the teachers make the class active and exciting. History focuses on leaders. As a leader I am eager to learn about other leaders.

Public speaking is another turn-on for me because I get a charge performing in front of a crowd. I gave my first stand-up speech when I was 12 years old, and I have been the master of ceremonies at many events. I frequently act as the emcee at girls' fashion shows and other local programs. I have a natural ability to do well in front of a group.

I am a good dancer and singer. My friends consider me the best dancer in school. To get a chance to perform, I started a rock band. I sing backup and dance in the band. Being in charge of things is a challenge. I have a chance to make things succeed, and I thrive on challenges. There is a risk that you may fail, but you also have an opportunity to succeed. Because I don't want to look bad to my friends, failure is not an option for me.

I make it in school because of my ability to develop good relationships with my teachers. Because I am active in so many things, I frequently ask for special favors such as being excused from class early. My teachers usually give me what I ask for.

Sometimes I am not able to establish a relationship with a teacher. When that happens I have a hard time learning. I remember very clearly one teacher I did not get along with. In my sophomore year I had a very passive geometry teacher who could not explain what geometry was all about. She was very bright, but she couldn't give the big picture or explain why geometry was important. I finally decided that if I was going to pass this class, I was going to have to teach myself. I did, and then I passed the class. I have to see what's in it for me and then I can learn. When teachers give all the details up front without giving a clear picture of what these things mean, I have difficulty learning. My geometry teacher had such distaste for me that when I turned in a perfect test paper, she accused me of cheating. She gave me a second test, and I aced that one, too. In that entire year, however, we never did communicate with each other because there was such a difference in styles.

Even though I am very bright and have a high IQ score, I can't use any brainpower if I don't see how a subject fits into real life. When I don't see the whole picture, I get frustrated quickly. When this happens I will do something dramatic to effect a change in the environment. What I mean by dramatic is that I may do something good or I may do something bad, but in any case I will attract attention. Most of the time, though, I am in control and laid back so usually I do something positive. For example, I may get up and ask a question to get the teacher to tell me a story explaining the material. On the negative side, I may pick an argument by expressing a different view or saying something like, "That's not what Dr. Jones said." If teachers back down I tend to bore in on them by saying, "You still haven't answered my question."

If I have a good relationship with a teacher, I can learn anything. If I don't have a good relationship, I have trouble learning anything. For example, I learned geometry in spite of my teacher, but it took a lot of energy on my part to do so. One more thing: I refuse to look bad, and I will do whatever it takes so that no one makes a fool of me. If a teacher is trying to make me look bad, I will spar with them. I am careful about who I pick a fight with, though. I don't pick a fight with someone if I can't win. I am good at one-liners and I use them to get even with people. I make sure I give these quips at the most opportune time so that I can cut people off at the knees and leave them with no comeback. I am attracted to this behavior because it is risky and because if I time the comments right I can leave people speechless. Timing in this is everything, and I have a natural ability to time my quips perfectly. I quickly learn how the game is played and how to win. Winning is important to me.

Although I like to socialize, I prefer to do my work alone unless I don't understand the material very well. If I am weak in a subject, I will get one friend who understands the material to work with me until I have learned it. After I know what I'm doing, then I prefer to work alone. Show me what you want me to do, lead me in the right direction, then leave me alone and let me do it. I don't want a lot of adult supervision because I can take care of myself. I don't really care a lot about grades except that together they act as kind of a scoreboard that lets you know how you are doing.

Classes in which I can make presentations are appealing to me. I don't do all that well on written tests, but if I can make an oral presentation I almost always get an A. Making presentations is a turn-on because I am in front of a group, and I can spice up the presentation with lots of stuff. Also, it is a physical event. I am moving around, and it is exciting to be up there. A lot of bright people in my class freeze up when they have to go up front of the class, but not me. Presenting to a group is one of my strengths. There is more risk involved, but there is an equal opportunity to look very good. In fact, my scenes are so good they make me look smarter than I really am.

I always wanted to be an adventurer like Marco Polo. In fact, I fantasize a lot about being part of an adventure. If teachers make classes exciting, it gives me a chance to be part of that adventure. I am lucky because I have always had good science teachers who made their subject stimulating.

In computer class I learn awesome information. Computers can do a lot of work for me and help me move down the road to get where I want to go. I look on math as a tool like an arrow in a quiver that you have to have in order to survive in the jungle. Once I understand a concept, though, I don't have to do 20 examples to prove I can do it.

Generally, English class is okay. The stories frequently are exciting, and there is a connection to communication, but I am not good at diagramming sentences. No one ever showed me why this is important, so I do not understand why we have to do it.

Field trips are cool. They are an adventure and a way to get out of class. The physical part of being kept in class all day is hard for me. If you want me to sit still for an hour in a confined space, I have to have some action along the way and see some payoff at the end. If you want me to accomplish some distant goal, give me rewards along the way. I get excited when I see what I can gain by doing a project, and I am willing to work as hard as necessary to do the job. If I don't see some personal gain in a project, I probably am not going to do any work. I don't need action and excitement all the time, just once in a while to keep me interested.

I spend at least as much time on extracurricular activities as I do on schoolwork. Playing sports, going to dances, and being in a band give me energy to get through the school day. I also am kind of an entrepreneur. I had a job after school 3 days a week. I did my job okay, but I was working for someone else and I wanted to be my own boss. In my spare time I started my own business selling CDs, jewelry, radios, and stuff on the web, to my classmates, and to some of my boss's customers. I was pretty successful, too. When my boss found out I had my own business on the side that competed with his, he fired me for taking away his customers. Because of this experience I don't want to work for other people. I want to be my own boss so I can do things my way. I do things differently than other people, but my way usually works out well. I am a bottom-line kind of guy. I am only interested in results. My attitude is "It's not how hard you work. It's how smart you work." I want to do things my way. Machiavelli was the real deal. The ends justify the means.

Although I tend to be a loner, I socialize with a lot of people and I have many friends at school. At least half of my close friends are girls. I enjoy their company and the fact that they have a different outlook on things. Some of my male friends can only talk about sports. They all talk the talk, but not too many of them walk the walk. The girls have interests besides sports, and because I am interested in many things, I am fascinated by the way girls think. Through my friendships with girls, I learned things that most of my male friends know very little about. For example, girls want you to talk, open up, and some want you to take charge of the situation. If there is one thing I can do, I can adapt to someone. With girls it is easy.

I go out a lot to parties and dancing. When I go out on a date I generally don't make plans. I let things happen as they will and take advantage of each situation. I go out with groups of people, but when I have a special date, I usually go out with just my date because she deserves my undivided attention. I probably have dated half of the girls in my class. I have no intention of getting serious with them and they know that. Even after I stop dating a girl, we still remain friends because I don't ever burn my bridges. In fact, I keep pictures of all of my friends, even girls I have stopped dating, and I look at them from time to time.

When I go out I intend to have a good time and be entertaining. Looking good in the eyes of others is important to me, so I dress in expensive or trendy clothes. Also, about once a month I take my date to an expensive restaurant where we can eat excellent food and dance. I always have money, so I can afford to go first class. When we are on a date, I frequently talk about my future. I share my dreams about what I want to accomplish in life and how I plan to get there. I fantasize about my future. I'm going to make it big. No punching time clocks for me.

Structure and routines stifle me and repetitive homework is the pits. I'm not a reader, I'm a doer, and I have a hard time memorizing things on a printed page. I prefer active classes where everyone has a part and plays it. That's how I learn outside of school, too. For example, when I make something, don't give me a blueprint to study. Let me watch and work with somebody until I learn how to do it.

In school I get along with everyone except for bullies. Bullies pick on kids who are weaker than they are, and I have no sympathy for people like that. Last year one kid was picking on some of the smaller kids, so I told him if he wanted to pick on someone he should pick on me. He made some comments to me, too, but I did not respond then. He was bigger than I was, so I waited until I could hit him when he was not looking. I caught him by surprise in the boys' room and shoved him against a wall and told him if he didn't stop picking on smaller kids I would be back. He stopped. There is no such thing as a fair fight. In a fight there is a winner and a loser. I do whatever I have to do to make sure I do not lose.

I always have my antennae out as I move about. When I first enter a room, I size up all the people in it to make sure that if there is trouble I can handle it. I don't expect trouble, but I want to be prepared just in case.

I usually eat dinner at home with my family because that is a good time to talk about things. My energy usually is low after a day in school so I spend the evening doing something active. For example, I get a charge out of training dogs, so I might take our German Shepherds out and practice obedience training. I almost always put off doing my homework until the last possible minute. That frequently means I don't do any homework at night. Instead, I make a deal with myself so I can do something active. I may have to get up half an hour early in the morning in order to get my homework done, but that is okay. That is the price of the deal I made with myself. Besides, morning is the time of day when I have the most energy.

CHARACTERISTICS OF PROMOTER STUDENTS

Promoters are resourceful, adaptable, and charming people who are action oriented (Kahler, 2000). They tend to act first without thinking about what they are going to do. Some of their strengths are their ability to be direct, to be decisive, to take action, and to run risks. Although they make up only 5% of the population in North America (Kahler, 1974), they make up nearly 12% of students who teachers identified as "most difficult" to teach, 14% of students who were labeled ADHD, hyperactive-impulsive type, and 16% of those who were labeled ADHD, inattentive type (Bailey, 1998). In North America, 60% of Promoters are male, and 40% are female (Kahler, 1974).

Promoters dress well and are trendsetters. They tend to like things that give a message of success. For this reason they like prestige products. As adults they own expensive cars (frequently red sports cars), wear expensive brand-name clothes, and eat in exclusive restaurants. As children they may prefer brand-name jeans, sneakers, shirts, and sunglasses. "If you've got it, flaunt it" might be their motto.

Many Promoters are kinesthetic learners who think best on their feet. Although they generally are laid back, they require spurts of action and excitement and are charged up by physical activity.

They have a hard time sitting still for long periods of time unless they are actively involved in projects that interest them. If they are interested in a subject, they will work very hard to accomplish the goals of the project. If they do not see any immediate benefit for themselves, they probably will have no interest in a subject and will have a very difficult time doing any work at all. They do not like rules, regimentation, routines, or boring work. Because most homework assignments are repetitive, Promoters hate homework assignments unless they are creative, exciting, stimulating, and adventuresome.

Because Promoters are persuasive and make friends easily, they have an ability to get others to do what they want them to do and so tend to be class leaders. They are motivated by excitement, and if they get their needs met positively they will be a positive influence. If they do not find an outlet for their energy and get into distress they can be a negative influence, leading fellow students in a negative direction or into disruptive behaviors (e.g., drugs, crime).

Promoters grow up fast. They tend to act like adults at an early age and want to be treated as adults. They want to do things their own way and do not want a lot of adult supervision. They are fearless thrill seekers who take on all challenges—the riskier the better. Although they like people, they are loners who form superficial relationships with many people but strong friendships with few. In spite of their need for excitement, they are laid-back individuals who usually keep themselves under control. If they get bored, feel threatened, or feel someone is putting them into an untenable situation or is trying to make them look bad, however, they may take aggressive action to turn the tables or to get revenge.

When Promoters enter a new environment they immediately "take the pulse" of a room and instinctively get a feel for how they can succeed in that environment. Forming positive relationships with teachers is extremely important to them and may be a crucial factor in how they view a class. Promoters like to win at anything they do. They do not like to fail, and if they do fail, they may blame their teachers for their failure. Because winning is so important to them, they may tell lies about other students or "con" other students into doing things that will get them in trouble.

Teaching Promoters can be challenging, exciting, rewarding, and fun for a teacher. Because Promoters like challenges, teachers can

Table 7.1. Promoter (Doer) need: Excitement

Help your Promoter students by
- Involving them in exciting projects
- Making sure directions are clear
- Letting them think on their feet
- Telling stories that instruct
- Finding ways to have them move around
- Using analogies that relate to other fields of their interest
- Telling sports and adventure stories
- Going on field trips
- Putting them in charge of something
- Sending them on errands and giving them a short lesson to do on the way
- Having them act, dance, sing, or mime a lesson
- Using games to get them involved
- Giving them as many different experiences as possible
- Presenting the big picture first and then moving to the details
- Quickly showing the practical application of the lesson first
- Breaking things up into short segments
- Providing a three-to-one ratio of application to theory
- Encouraging them to participate in sports or other exciting activities
- Giving them immediate, tangible rewards for accomplishments or jobs well done
- Letting them do an impersonation for the class
- Challenging them to accomplish something in each class
- Giving short-term rewards along the way on lengthy assignments
- Making deals with them
- Giving clear, concise directions

From Kahler, T. (1982). *Personality pattern inventory validation studies.* Little Rock, AR: Kahler Communications, Inc., and Kahler, T. (1996). *Personality pattern inventory.* Little Rock, AR: Kahler Communications, Inc.; adapted by permission.

reach them by challenging them in exciting and creative ways. Teachers also can reach Promoter students by including some exciting or competitive activities in every lesson, by presenting the big picture first, and by tying instruction to practical application in real life. Because Promoters like to make deals, even with themselves, teachers can keep them motivated and working on task by making deals with them; by giving them specific short-term, achievable goals; and by providing short-term rewards. Because Promoters are "now" people, immediate perks are better than future rewards. For adult Promoters, a bonus today is much better than a 401(k) plan. For child Promoters an immediate, short-term reward is better than an A at the end of the marking period. (See Table 7.1 for other ideas to help the Promoter student.)

A TEACHER'S STORY

This story demonstrates miscommunication between a Workaholic teacher and a Promoter student who is in distress. By shifting to the student's preferred channel of communication and keeping the student actively engaged in lessons, the teacher enabled the student to succeed in class and greatly reduced his negative behaviors.

At 17 years of age, Jason is a charming young man. He is bright, engaging, and always excited about something. He loves to help with class demonstrations and to be the center of attention. His classmates seem to enjoy his enthusiasm in various classroom projects. Thanks to these qualities, he can be a real asset to learning in the classroom.

I didn't always know the best ways to approach Jason, however. At the beginning of the school year before I had gotten to know him, I found him to be quite a challenge. When I would review material, he would impulsively shout out the answers. Asking him to think before he spoke had no impact on him. I tried to carefully explain the material so the students would be comfortable moving on. Most of the students quietly took notes, listened, and asked a few questions. Jason, on the other hand, fidgeted and talked to his neighbors, asking them if they were as bored as he was. When I would give him "the look," he always responded with, "What am I doing? I wasn't doing anything." His behavior was exasperating and disruptive, but I couldn't help feeling that maybe I had not made the material as exciting as it could be.

The clincher came one day when Jason had been especially disruptive, and constant reminders to him to be quiet (and his responding protests) caused me to lose my train of thought several times. The class was to last 90 minutes with a 10-minute break in between. As the students filed out for their break, I quickly looked at the remainder of my lesson plan and began reorganizing it.

The first thing I decided to do was to place Jason near the front of the class. This would serve two purposes: one, I could monitor his behavior better, and two, I could have him help me with a series of tasks. I decided I would administer a quick self-test for the students to assess their understanding of the unit. Then, I would have them break into groups and give them a series of manipulatives and games for further reinforcement. Each group would cover a different topic. Every 10 minutes, the groups would switch to a different station. I knew that Jason had to be busy, active, and engaged. As the students returned to class, I gave them the self-assessment and took Jason aside. I told him in a clear, firm voice that I was counting on him to do several things during the class, and in order to do them he would need to sit near the front. I instructed him to go to the closet to get the manipulatives and games and bring them to me. As I formed the groups, he was to place one set of materials at each of their tables. I told him to join a group, but he would also have the job of timekeeper. Every 10 minutes he was to instruct the other students to switch groups.

Jason's response was very positive, and he followed all directions given. As he left that day I thanked him for his help. He seemed genuinely pleased and asked if he could be exempted from the homework since he had done so well. I thought for a moment and said, "Do the homework for tonight and bring it to me before class tomorrow so I can check it. Then you can be the 'teacher' and correct it with the rest of the class tomorrow." Using the Directive channel with Jason and giving him the opportunity to be at the front of the class leading his classmates gave him the motivation he needed for doing the homework. After that, as long I kept him engaged and offered him active pursuits for at least part of the period, his disruptions significantly decreased and we developed a positive relationship for the rest of the year.

Many teachers have Promoter as one of the least well-developed parts of their personality structure. Consequently, they have a problem communicating with and motivating their Promoter students. In this instance, the Workaholic teacher decided to develop assignments that would allow Jason to move around periodically and to keep him involved in various activities in order to meet his needs for excitement and action. She also shifted to Jason's favorite channel of communication, the Directive channel, to make sure he knew exactly what was expected of him. These strategies worked, and the teacher and Jason had a productive relationship for the rest of the school year.

ADAPT, SURVIVE, AND MAKE THINGS HAPPEN!

AN OUNCE
OF
PREVENTION

HOW
PROCESS
COMMUNICATION
INTEGRATES
WITH
OTHER
LEARNING
THEORIES

CHAPTER 8

One of the most useful aspects of the Process Communication Model (PCM) is how well it fits with other learner-centered approaches to instruction. Educators are expected to incorporate methods such as Multiple Intelligences, various learning-style strategies, brain-based learning, cooperative learning, and peer tutoring into their teaching. PCM complements all of these means of delivering instruction.

MULTIPLE INTELLIGENCES

In 1983, Howard Gardner, a renowned Harvard University researcher, provided a way to map the broad range of abilities that all students possess through the identification of seven (now eight) areas of capabilities that he defined as intelligences. He called his theory "Multiple Intelligences" (MI). Just as everyone has parts of all six personality types of varying strengths in them, they also have all eight intelligences, though some are more well developed than others. Schools have traditionally measured student success through only two of these intelligences: linguistic and logical/mathematical. Those who tend to be weak or deficient in those areas are often labeled *learning disabled.* The other intelligences identified by Gardner, however, open up a wider range of teaching, learning, and assessment possibilities that can reach more students than traditional instruction. Many educators have adopted Gardner's theories as a regular part of their classroom teaching.

Armstrong (1994) recommended incorporating MI into lesson-plan design in order to reach the wide array of students found in today's classrooms. He stated, "MI theory opens the door to a wide variety of teaching strategies that can be easily implemented in the classroom" (p. 65). Kahler and educators who use PCM recommend designing lessons so that they incorporate activities that meet the motivational needs of each personality type (Bradley & Smith, 1999; Jackson & Pauley, 1999; Kahler, 1995). Teachers who design activities that incorporate the eight intelligences into their lessons are likely to teach to the strengths of each of their students. When these activities also address the needs of each personality type as identified by Kahler (see Chapter 1, Table 1.4), it is more likely that students will be fully engaged in the learning process. The eight intelligences that Gardner recognized are as follows:

1. *Linguistic* (word smart): a capacity to effectively use words orally or in writing

2. *Logical/mathematical* (number smart): the capacity to use numbers effectively, such as categorization, classification, calculation, and hypothesis testing

3. *Spatial* (picture smart): the ability to perceive visual–spatial concepts such as color, line, shape, form, space, and the relationships among them

4. *Bodily-kinesthetic* (body smart): expertise in using the body to express ideas, feelings, and talents such as athletics, dexterity, flexibility, and speed

5. *Musical* (music smart): the ability to perceive or perform music and rhythms

6. *Interpersonal* (people smart): a capacity to know and respond effectively to other people

7. *Intrapersonal* (self smart): the ability to know oneself and the awareness of how that affects intentions, motivations, and desires

8. *Naturalistic* (nature smart): expertise in relating to various forms of nature, such as plant and animal kingdoms and their relationship to the natural world

For instance, for the unit "Protecting the Rain Forests," Table 8.1 shows classroom activities that meet the needs of all personality types and simultaneously address Gardner's eight intelligences. Students could be allowed to select the projects on which they would work. Dioramas capitalize on the artistic talents of Rebels, keep Promoters busy with their hands, allow the Naturalist to depict a scene in nature, and use the talents of the student whose strength is in spatial orientation. In addition, the Dreamer can contemplate the overall layout and is good at gathering and designing the parts of the scene. A song or rap with gestures taps into musical as well as kinesthetic abilities, takes advantage of the creativity of the Rebel, and keeps the Promoter involved and center stage. Workaholics and Persisters as well as others with strong linguistic intelligence enjoy gathering and presenting facts through research. Workaholics and

Table 8.1. Class activities designed by learning style and personality type

Activity	Intelligence	Personality type
Design a diorama that depicts the current state of the rain forest.	Spatial Naturalistic	Rebel Promoter Dreamer
Write and perform a song or rap with gestures about ways to protect the rain forests.	Musical Kinesthetic	Rebel Promoter
Research and prepare a written or oral report that includes the location of the rain forests and reasons for their current condition.	Linguistic	Workaholic Persister
Gather and graph data on at least five changing conditions in the rain forest.	Mathematical	Workaholic Persister
Work in a group to find out how protecting the rain forests will affect humans and animals.	Interpersonal	Reactor
Design an individual project depicting ways in which to protect the rain forests.	Intrapersonal	Dreamer Promoter

Persisters with mathematical talent are able to synthesize, classify, and depict the information through graphs and charts. Reactors and those with strong interpersonal strengths enjoy working in groups and will be motivated to find out how protecting the rain forest affects others. Those who excel in knowing themselves well (intrapersonal intelligence) often prefer to contemplate their own ideas and then to create a project to which they can relate. This is a good activity for Dreamers, who also need some time to contemplate, as well as for Promoters, who like an opportunity to work independently.

LEARNING STYLES

Learning styles are preferred ways of understanding, thinking, and processing information. Several learning style theories assess different aspects of the cognitive process. The most widely used learning style theory, developed by Bandler (1988) and Grinder, is that of separating the learning process into visual, auditory, and tactile/kinesthetic modes of input and response. In the course of a school day, students are asked not only to take in information but also to express what they know. If teachers present materials visually, auditorially, and kinesthetically, and if they let students show what they have learned through these modes, they may find that students know more than originally anticipated.

Workaholics and Persisters tend to be auditory learners, although they incorporate the other modalities as well. They are comfortable listening to lectures, gathering data, synthesizing oral information, and participating in discussions. They are usually good at taking organized notes and remembering what they hear. Reactors also enjoy discussions, especially in small groups with their peers, but also respond to visually appealing forms of learning. Dreamers respond best to tactile tasks such as handiwork and computer programming; they also tend to do better when assignments are structured and written down for them. Learning is more relevant and exciting for Rebels and Promoters who prefer the kinesthetic mode when they can learn with their bodies, move around, and have contact with others. Being able to actually perform an experiment, use a computer program, or build a model is the best way for them to hold on to information.

Environmental, emotional, psychological, and personal connections also are important learning style factors to consider. Reactors need their classroom environment to reflect and provide comfort through sensory input. They have a primary need to connect to the curriculum through their feelings and emotions. They are interested in how the subject matter they are studying affects other people and society. Psychological and emotional factors also are of primary importance to Persisters, who filter what is learned through their values, attitudes, and belief systems.

The relationship between the instructor and student is important to Reactors, Persisters, Promoters, and Rebels. Reactors learn better when they have a warm relationship with teachers who they know care about them. Persisters need to build a relationship of trust, credibility, and respect to make learning meaningful to them and to take seriously what teachers are teaching them. Promoters will work hard for a teacher they like and respect, and if a teacher can inject some humor into the class, Rebels can make a personal connection and are encouraged to perform well. Workaholics, on the other hand, consider the content of utmost importance; even if the learner dislikes the teacher, learning will likely still take place. Personal relationships and contact are not so important to Dreamers—

they relate better to ideas, materials, and mechanical devices and may enjoy observing relationships more than participating in them.

Still other learning style factors affect a student's ability to be receptive to information presented in the classroom. One of these factors is concrete versus abstract. Concrete learners prefer to learn through objects and things that can be handled, manipulated, and touched. They like to try things out and prefer games, movement, and learning through hands-on activities. Rebels and Promoters tend to be concrete learners. They need to experience learning and see the relevance to their lives. Workaholics, Persisters, Dreamers, and Reactors usually learn better through more abstract modes such as books, words, ideas, and conversations. Dreamers can find solitude in the world of books and words, while Reactors love to discuss and talk with others about ideas and people.

Another factor to consider is whether the student learns best *actively* or *reflectively*. Active learners such as Rebels and Promoters learn by doing. They need to dive right in and take immediate action to experience the subject. They enjoy experiments and keep doing something until they figure it out. Reflective learners such as Dreamers respond internally. They take in information and reflect on all possibilities before taking any action. They often stand on the fringes and passively watch what others are doing.

Workaholics and Persisters prefer working with partners or alone. They like to set their own timetables, pursue research at their own rate, and put their own name on their product. These types tend to be internally motivated. Dreamers also prefer to work alone but may need more external stimulation and direction in order to accomplish a task. They also need the task broken down into small "chunks." Promoters also need external motivation and prefer to be on the fringes of the group or a member of many groups, but not necessarily committed to a specific project unless it is of their own undertaking. The Assessing Matrix for Educators (Figure 8.1) shows the best ways in which to reach each of the types.

Most often, teachers present material in their own most comfortable learning style. The key to communicating effectively and reaching all learners is to vary teaching modes as well as assessment techniques. Offering both variety and choice so that students can "multiprocess" gives them the widest array of possibilities for learning.

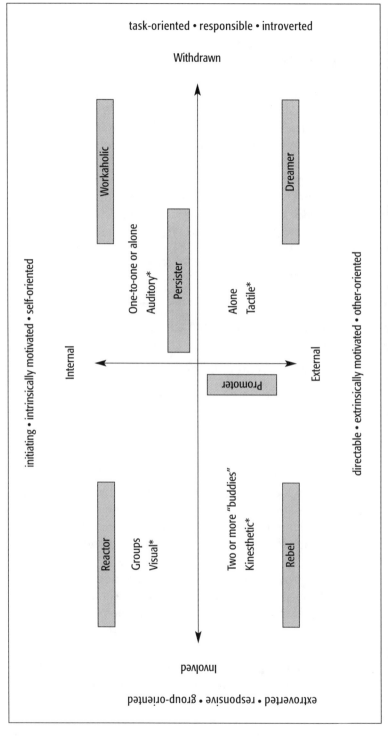

Figure 8.1. The Assessing Matrix, showing preferred instruction style and motivations of each personality type. (From Kahler, T. [1979]. *Process therapy in brief.* Little Rock, AR: Human Development Publications; adapted by permission.)

*Dr. Okie Wolfe has suggested the correlation of these learning styles.

107

BRAIN-BASED LEARNING

New instructional paradigms based on brain research are changing the way in which instruction is delivered. Brain-based research tells us that "growing a smart brain requires the exploration of alternative methods, multiple answers, critical thinking, and creative insights" (Jensen, 1995, p. 19). Humans need to create a personal model for the information they learn; therefore, a number of factors need to be taken into consideration for maximum learning to occur. Researchers who have studied brain-based optimal learning conditions tell us to consider the following issues when designing learning activities:

• Responding to multiple intelligences

• Input of the five senses (especially visual, auditory, and tactile)

• Learning preferences (left/right brain hemispheres; abstract or concrete)

• Personal history and present circumstances of our students

• Relevance to the daily lives of our students

Three major learning areas of the brain are 1) *cognitive* (i.e., what we know), which includes recall, comprehension, application, comparison, synthesis, and analysis; 2) *affective* (i.e., what we feel), which includes values, attitudes, participation, and feelings; and 3) *psychomotor* (i.e., what we do), which are physical skills of coordination and manipulation. Students learn best when all three of these areas can be addressed within a lesson or unit so that neural connections can be made in a holistic manner incorporating mind, heart, and body.

There are many ways to make neural connections in the brain to help students learn and remember material. Some of these are: graphic organizers, paraphrasing, mnemonic devices, peer teaching, student-generated questions, summarizing, role-playing, debating, outlining, timelines, bulletin boards, costumes, color-coding, movement, music, games, reenactments, storytelling, and discussion groups. As can be seen in Table 8.2, these techniques tend to appeal to different personality types, although there are some that all will enjoy! If all of these learning activities are included at some point in the instructional process and/or students are given choices as to how

Table 8.2. Learning activities suited to each personality type

Type	Learning activity
Reactor	Graphic organizers, storytelling, peer teaching, bulletin boards, costumes, discussion groups
Workaholic	Paraphrasing, graphic organizers, mnemonics, student-generated questions, outlining, timelines, discussion groups
Persister	Paraphrasing, mnemonics, peer teaching, student-generated questions, debates, discussion groups
Dreamer	Graphic organizers, summarizing, outlining, color coding
Rebel	Mnemonics, role-playing, bulletin boards, costumes, color-coding, movement, music, games, reenactments
Promoter	Peer teaching, student-generated questions, role-playing, debates, movement, games, reenactments, storytelling

they can receive and express their knowledge, they are more likely to be successful.

Most classrooms and standardized assessments tend to focus on memorization; however, our brains are actually poorly designed for rote learning (Jensen, 1995). The brain learns best when many of the neurological pathways are stimulated at the same time.

Therefore, classrooms that are "noisy, busy, and provide choices for learners" (Jensen, 1995, p. 25); include field trips and other real-life activities; have personal meaning; and tap into emotions are the ones that help students connect knowledge and maximize learning.

COOPERATIVE LEARNING

Cooperative learning is finding popularity in many classrooms today. It is based on cooperative instructional strategies that incorporate interaction among students as part of the learning process. Many cooperative learning structures focus on student-to-student consulting, mastery of curriculum, enhancement of thinking skills, and participation in specialized roles and tasks through teamwork (Kagan, 1994).

When cooperative learning is incorporated into a lesson or unit, students are given the opportunity to develop and reinforce their

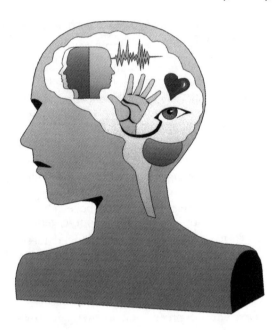

skills with partners, groups, or teams. Reactors benefit the most from cooperative learning. Strategies most helpful to these individuals are those that enable them to feel that they are a part of the group, work with others, bounce ideas off their peers, and be members of a team. Friendships and memberships are the essence of what they consider important in life, and connecting these to a form of learning enhances their ability to grasp facts and concepts.

Dreamers also benefit from cooperative learning structures when the group is not too large and when roles and responsibilities are clearly delineated. This design automatically structures the assignment for them, and the other members of the group can help the Dreamer focus and stay on task. It is much harder to get lost in a group of four or five than in a whole class!

For a group that contains Persisters and Workaholics, it is important that roles and responsibilities be clearly defined as well; otherwise, these individuals tend to take over the group and want to do all the work themselves. Workaholics can be given leadership roles and tasks that capitalize on their organizational skills and their sense of responsibility. When teachers ensure that Persisters understand the purpose for the assignment and get their support for the project, students of this type can often help the group stay motivated.

Promoters and Rebels also enjoy cooperative structures, which provide them with more peer contact and idea-sharing as well as more opportunities to take on leadership roles within the group. In many cooperative activities, outcomes include some type of hands-on project and large-group presentations. These types of activities are appealing to both Rebels and Promoters and meet their needs for fun and excitement in the classroom. Promoters like it when they know their role and can have some individual time to go off and prepare on their own. In addition, they rise to the challenge of making sure that everyone in the group knows the material. Both Rebels and Promoters enjoy the role of presenter when the team shares their project with the class. There are many more opportunities for Rebels and Promoters to get their needs met in cooperative groups than in traditional lecture, writing, or reading activities.

The cooperative structure, Team Word Webbing (Kagan, 1994), illustrates a learning arrangement that meets the needs of each personality type. In this activity, each group of five students is given a large sheet of paper and a different color marker for each group member. The task is to brainstorm ideas for "Motivation for the Westward Movement." This topic is written in a circle in the middle of the

paper. Then, each member contributes to a "web" of reasons for people moving west in the nineteenth century. Several group members can write at once, and they can "branch" off on each other's ideas. When the task is complete, students sign their names in their assigned color. The team must then think of a way for all group members to participate in sharing their web (e.g., two students can hold up the paper while the other three read the ideas). The teacher can immediately see who participated by looking at the colors of the contributions.

In this type of cooperative activity, in addition to learning, each personality type can find their "niche." Reactors enjoy the group process. Workaholics are likely to contribute many ideas while Persisters can help keep everyone on task. Rebels get a chance to draw and see the ideas in different colors. Promoters like to manipulate the markers, may be motivated by the challenge to come up with ideas, and will enjoy sharing the finished product with the class. Dreamers can take their time, look at the ideas of others, and build on those. This is just one of many cooperative learning structures in which students can participate that include something for every personality type.

PEER TEACHING

Students from kindergarten through high school enjoy teaching and tutoring others. Peer teaching can take several forms. Many peer teaching models focus on older students tutoring younger students or more able students tutoring those who need help or who have missed learning. Yet another model, classwide peer tutoring, is an instructional arrangement that involves reciprocal tutoring. All have a research base that shows positive academic outcomes in both elementary and secondary programs. The possibilities for student-to-student teaching are endless and incorporate the most abundant, economical, and motivated resource we have in our schools—the students themselves (Bradley & Graves, 1997).

Let's take a look at how each of the six personality types might respond to participating in a peer teaching model:

- Reactors love to help and be needed. Peer teaching provides the perfect vehicle for them to interact with their peers in a help-

ing role, as well as to establish a close, positive relationship with someone.

- Workaholics usually accomplish all tasks required of them in a timely manner. Peer tutoring offers them a vehicle to share what they know with others. In addition, the organizational and responsibility factors involved in teaching others tap into their strength areas.

- Persisters often have strong beliefs regarding helping others and hold the value that students should do their best work. Peer tutoring offers them the opportunity to perform a valuable service to others as well as to share their values of persistence and hard work.

- Dreamers benefit from peer tutoring in a variety of ways. Being in the tutoring role requires them to have learned the material well enough to teach it to someone else. As the one being tutored, the Dreamer benefits from instruction that is one-to-one and that enables him or her to work more at his or her own pace.

- Rebels enjoy the face-to-face contact and undivided attention that peer tutoring affords. They can usually come up with creative ideas for helping others learn. It is easier for them to stay on task, the pace of instruction is geared more to their attention span, and there is no "down time" in which to become distracted.

- Promoters like to be the center of attention and the person in charge, so being a peer tutor helps to add to their feelings of importance. Having to tutor another student provides motivation for the Promoter to master the material. They can be a positive influence on their peers when given the opportunity to lead in a productive way.

Peer teaching offers students many opportunities to work with partners who are on the same level in such subjects as vocabulary, comprehension, and content reading. Within the same classroom, students who are functioning at a higher level can tutor students who are having difficulty or who are at a lower academic level. Cross-age tutoring can occur within a school among classes of lower and upper grades. In addition, middle and high school students who are required to perform community service in order to graduate may choose to tutor same-age peers or younger students. When given the responsibility to participate in someone else's learning, many individuals who are experiencing some sort of difficulty in their own school situation, such as learning and/or behavior problems, often show improvement in these areas. Moreover, cross-age friendships, role modeling, and friendships with students with disabilities often occur. Peer teaching provides for the enhancement of students' academic and social progress in the school setting and can serve as a way to reach each of the six personality types.

CONCLUSION

Educators are constantly learning new strategies and constructs for teaching and learning. We have examined some of these that are in use in many school systems such as multiple intelligences, learning styles, brain-based learning, cooperative learning, and peer teaching. When teachers are able to interface Kahler's personality types along with the implementation of these procedures, learning and achievement can be greatly enhanced. As students get their needs met through a variety of instructional formats, they will be happier and more productive learners.

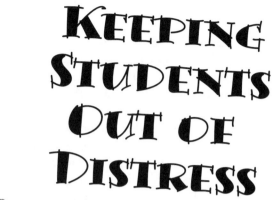

KEEPING STUDENTS OUT OF DISTRESS

CHAPTER 9

"Emotional well-being is the strongest predictor of achievement in school and on the job," said C.R. Pool (1997, p. 12). Clearly, for students to make learning a priority, they must feel safe from both physical and emotional harm. When students are subjected to real or perceived intimidation, rejection, embarrassment, or inadequacy, they tend to respond either by acting out or withdrawing—and learning is unlikely to occur. When students focus their energies on figuring out ways to cope with their stress, their ability to think and remember is impaired. Conversely, when their psychological needs are met, students tend to perform well in school. In fact, students learn best when an activity is meaningful, that is, when they can connect it to getting their emotional needs met. "When those needs are met in the classroom, students want to learn and to achieve to the highest standards," noted Rogers and Renard (1999, p. 34). Thus, reducing the stress that students feel in the classroom is essential to learning.

When students do not get their needs met, they become distressed. Students can become stressed over a variety of situations occurring at home (e.g., divorce, poverty, crowded living conditions) and in school (e.g., test anxiety, lack of friends, being teased or left out); the stress may even be self-induced (e.g., guilt, shame, feelings of inadequacy). When students don't find ways to get their needs met positively, they will find negative ways. Certain negative behaviors are exhibited by each type of student when he or she is in distress in the classroom.

We have all seen the ways in which students display negative behaviors to get certain needs met. Rebels may wear provocative clothes and have body piercings in order to be noticed by their classmates and to get negative attention from adults. Promoters can become argumentative with teachers when told to follow the rules and often set up power struggles so they can get excitement going in the classroom. Workaholics in distress get disgusted with their cooperative learning groups and angrily take home all the work to do themselves. Persisters may actively criticize the contributions of their classmates, whereas Reactors put themselves down and may cry when they make mistakes. Dreamers check out, stare out the window, and accomplish nothing.

When teachers know the personality types of their students and observe them engaged in distress behaviors indicative of that type, they can immediately apply their knowledge of preferred channels of communication and also utilize their ability to identify the unmet needs of each type (see Chapter 1). When armed with this information, employing positive interventions becomes more manageable and successful for educators. Sometimes a student might simply need a jump-start—one small circumstance or event to meet their needs. It might be a friendly greeting, a high five, or being sent on an errand. Some teachers use a lesson introduction that gives a "battery charge" to all of the personality types (see Chapter 10). Rebels, Promoters, and Dreamers often have a long history of not getting their needs met in school, however, and may require more long-term interventions.

Today's classrooms are filled with students of diverse types and needs. Just as these students respond to stress in different ways, what appeals to one may be a "turn-off" to another. For instance, some students appear to dismiss stress; others consider it a challenge and rise to the occasion; still others shut down. By understanding students' various perspectives, teachers can more successfully foster engagement in the learning process (Dodd, 1995). A variety of teaching approaches and instructional styles enhance the atmosphere of the classroom and provide opportunities for multiple modes of learning and creative outlets of production. When teachers are able to align their instruction with student needs and preferences, more learning takes place (Wubbels, Levy, & Brekelmans, 1997).

Each type of student may experience stress in a different way, leading to a different set of responses. According to Dr. Kahler (2000), there are three degrees of distress. All of us and all of our students experience first-degree distress (the lowest level) many times during the day. It may be when a student is called on to answer a problem out loud, when a young man sees a pretty girl in the hallway, or when someone else gets chosen for a coveted classroom job. Awareness of the signals that each type exhibits in first-degree distress can help the teacher know how to intervene before major problems ensue.

Second-degree distress is more noticeable and can often be disruptive to student and classroom learning. Some students manifest this distress by acting out in class. They may shout at the teacher, hit classmates, or throw chairs. Others may verbally attack classmates or their teachers or engage in negative drama by making fools of classmates or teachers. Still others may get depressed and shut down or get nervous and make silly mistakes on things they already know how to do. When teachers observe specific distress behaviors and are aware of interventions that invite each type of student out of distress, more time can be devoted to teaching and learning.

When students of any type are in third-degree distress, it is evident by their lack of motivation and the depths of their despair. All students in third-degree distress feel depressed, unloved, unwanted, and useless. They may appear listless and lose interest in schoolwork or in life itself. They may stop caring about their appearance, their work, or any activities. Their despair may be so deep that they may conclude that life is not worth living. These students may require intense intervention to get their needs met.

How can we identify when students are in distress? What techniques are available for inviting them out of it or preventing them from becoming distressed in the first place? Awareness of the early signs of distress provides the knowledge and opportunity to intervene before major problems result (Kahler, 2000).

REACTORS

Everyone is working individually in class on an important assignment. The teacher is coming around to check the students' work. One student is getting nervous; she can't remember any of the answers. She erases an answer for the third time and makes a hole in her paper. She laughs at herself nervously and says, "I am so stupid." Then she begins to cry.

What Do Reactors in Distress Look Like?

Reactors have a need to please everyone. If there is disharmony, they can become immobilized and have difficulty making decisions because someone might be displeased. Another sign of Reactors in first-degree distress is a constant need for reassurance, which might be manifested in someone who laughs inappropriately at him- or herself. If a person acts sad, worried, confused, or inadequate and makes mistakes on things he or she already knows how to do, it is

a signal that an individual is entering second-degree distress mode. Reactor students may become clumsy and careless and do things such as fall, spill things, and bump into things, whereas typically they would be quite coordinated. They also tend to make denigrating comments about themselves when they feel they have done something stupid. Because Reactors usually care a great deal about how they look, a clear sign that they are in distress is when their appearance deteriorates.

How Can We Get Reactors Out of Distress?

Telling Reactors they did a good job on an assignment is much less important than telling them "I'm glad you're here." They like to feel important and needed. Selecting them to be a buddy for a new student or to be in charge of the class party helps them feel that they are a necessary part of the school and ties into their strength of nurturing others. Writing personal comments on papers to accompany grades lets them feel a personal connection with the teacher. Making positive comments on their appearance or their personal life demonstrates unconditional caring.

Reactors also need sensory satisfaction. They are very aware of their environment—who likes whom, what people are wearing, how things look, and what colors go together. They prefer a cozy and attractive classroom. Inviting them to take care of or fix up the room in some way capitalizes on their aesthetic strengths. Selecting them for the care of classroom plants and animals and making sure they have opportunities to work with others can keep Reactors out of distress.

One of the most important questions that an educator can ask him- or herself when a student is in distress is this: What channel do I use with this personality type? The Reactor responds best to the Nurturative channel. Talking in a soft, nurturing voice and creating a classroom environment conducive to sharing feelings and ideas helps Reactors feel comfortable and available for learning.

Setting Up the Classroom for Reactors

The classroom should be an inviting place with colorful bulletin boards, a warm, cozy reading corner, and colorful artwork neatly displayed. Stuffed animals, a beanbag chair, plants, and posters of famous people make the room warm and appealing for the Reactor. Games that provide physical contact, such as the Crazy Handshake (Loomans & Kolberg, 1995), give the Reactor an appropriate opportunity to make physical and social contact with others, which is very important to their well-being. Table 9.1 presents many of the behaviors, needs, channels, and preventions/interventions that apply to Reactors in distress.

WORKAHOLICS

The class is working in teams on an assignment. Suddenly, one of the students calls one of his team members "stupid" and says, "Give me that paper. You are all so dumb you don't see how to do anything. Let me do it."

Table 9.1. The Reactor in distress

Behaviors	Can't make decisions
	Puts self down
	Needs constant reassurance to complete work
	Tugs on teacher to get attention
	Laughs inappropriately at self
	Inserts "you know" inappropriately
	Needs to please
	Makes "klutzy" mistakes on things he or she knows how to do
	Is clumsy, careless—falls, spills things, bumps into things
	Becomes immobilized if disharmony occurs
	Gets uptight taking tests
	Acts sad, worried, confused, inadequate
	Lets appearance deteriorate
	Cries easily
	Gets physically ill if disharmony persists
Needs	Recognition for person
	Sensory
Channel	Nurturative
Preventions/ interventions	Use Nurturative channel
	Provide welcome to class ("I'm glad you're here")
	Make personal comments (on papers and verbally)
	Select to decorate bulletin board
	Provide opportunities to work with others (cooperative learning, peer tutors)
	Select to care for plants/animals in classroom
	Provide comfortable places to work/read in the class
	Select as host/hostess for parties
	Ask to serve as a buddy for new students

From Kahler, T. (1982). *Personality pattern inventory validation studies.* Little Rock, AR: Kahler Communications, Inc., and Kahler, T. (1995). *The Process Teaching Seminar.* Little Rock, AR: Kahler Communications, Inc.; adapted by permission.

What Do Workaholics in Distress Look Like?

During classroom discussions Workaholics in first-degree distress easily become impatient with others and tend to call out answers. They expect perfection of themselves and often become frustrated

when others don't work toward doing their best. Workaholics can be very rigid about time. They become upset when the schedule changes, and they are usually the first ones to tell a substitute exactly when and how each event is supposed to take place (e.g., what time to start each subject, how to take attendance, who is in charge of what). They want things to be fair and orderly. Workaholics can become obsessive about getting grades and credit for all of their work. They are the ones who will ask, "Is this on the test?"

When Workaholics move into second-degree distress they tend to overcontrol. Behaviors having to do with order, cleanliness, and possessions become overexaggerated. They may not want to participate in art activities that are "messy" and often will not share their supplies because others may not have the same respect for order that they do. During group work they might take over the group—telling everyone else what to do, becoming impatient with others, and maybe even doing all the work themselves because no one else can do it better, faster, or more efficiently. They become extremely frustrated with others who don't think the same way as they do (in a logical, organized, efficient fashion). They might verbally attack someone for not thinking clearly or for doing something "stupid."

How Can We Get Workaholics Out of Distress?

Workaholics need recognition for work. When teachers give them positive compliments about their ideas, accomplishments, organizational skills, or perseverance, it helps reduce their distress. Workaholics also respond well to mechanisms for time-structuring. Teachers should make sure that Workaholic students know the schedule and stick to it. They can also provide these students with organizational tools such as syllabi, rubrics, and/or daily plans to help them feel more secure about being able to successfully accomplish their assigned tasks on time. Advanced organizers such as word or story webs help them organize their thoughts.

For the Workaholic, the preferred communication channel is the Requestive. Asking Workaholic students who, what, where, when, and how questions can jump-start their thinking process and put them in their comfort zone. *Asking* them if they will do something instead of ordering them to do it is a helpful technique to use with Workaholics.

Setting Up the Classroom for Workaholics

A classroom that has a prominent space for honored work to be displayed will appeal to a Workaholic. Schools that provide assignment books and calendars win over their Workaholic students (although more than likely they will buy their own if these are not provided!). Making sure that students receive letter grades for their work as well as positive comments and even tangible rewards such as certificates for a job well done will keep Workaholic students motivated. Providing time for them to tutor other students is one way to recognize them for their hard work and accomplishments and shows them that their skills are valued. Table 9.2 presents many of the behaviors, needs, channels, and preventions/interventions that apply to Workaholics in distress.

Table 9.2. The Workaholic in distress

Behaviors	Overcontrols—takes over groups
	Rigid about time and schedule changes
	Tells others what to do
	Does others' work for them
	Takes on too much work
	Does not delegate well
	Gets frustrated with others who don't think the same
	Has issues regarding order, cleanliness, money
	Expects perfection of self
	Excessively erases or redoes work to get it perfect
	Calls out answers
	Criticizes others' answers
	Excessively asks "Does this count toward our grade?" "Is this on the test?"
	Uses big words when small words would be clearer
	Inserts parenthetical expressions in statements
Needs	Recognition for work
	Time structure
Channel	Requestive
Preventions/ Interventions	Use Requestive channel
	Give positive comments about work
	Give positive public recognition for achievements
	Display work
	Give tangible rewards for work
	Give letter grades
	Select as peer tutor
	Provide schedules
	Use assignment books and calendars
	Provide organizational structure (e.g., syllabus)
	Keep to time commitments
	Select for distinctive academic opportunities

From Kahler, T. (1982). *Personality pattern inventory validation studies.* Little Rock, AR: Kahler Communications, Inc., and Kahler, T. (1995). *The Process Teaching Seminar.* Little Rock, AR: Kahler Communications, Inc.; adapted by permission.

PERSISTERS

The class is working on an assignment when one student says to another in a loud voice, "Stop copying off my paper." The second student tells him to stop bugging him and get off his back. The first student then launches into a diatribe about the importance of doing your own work and following the rules. When the teacher tells the students to be quiet, the first student turns away in indignation.

What Do Persisters in Distress Look Like?

The student who is constantly finding fault with others (tattling, putting others down) is probably a Persister in first-degree distress. They tend to be self-righteous and are overly sensitive to negative feedback because of their compulsive need to be right. Persisters who are in distress often erase or edit their work over and over in

order to get it perfect, thereby producing a very imperfect product! You may see them rolling their eyes when others say something they consider stupid, and if you hear the words "you should," they are usually connected to a Persister who is agitated.

As they move into second-degree distress, they display rigidity about "the right way" (my way) and are often critical of others. They are especially critical of other students when they do not follow the rules, lack commitment and dedication, and do not care about things that are important to the Persister. When under pressure, they often become argumentative about their ideas. They feel it is their duty to tell others what to do, and when their directions aren't followed, they can get sarcastic and inflexible. They become upset when others do not believe in or respect their convictions, and it is difficult for them to see two sides of an issue. Equity is important to Persisters, and when they are distressed, they become overly concerned with rules and fairness. Table 9.3 presents many of the behaviors, needs, channels, and preventions/interventions that apply to Persisters in distress.

How Can We Get Persisters Out of Distress?

Asking Persisters to share their views, positions, and opinions motivates them and acknowledges that their ideas are important. Giving Persisters leadership roles in the classroom capitalizes on one of their key strengths and allows them to engage in activities that they consider valuable. Providing them with opportunities to engage in service projects reinforces their dedication and commitment to worthwhile endeavors.

Persisters appreciate recognition for their work, although they often know when they have done a good job and, rather than basing their worth on the teacher's opinion, they merely need his or her verification. Recognizing Persisters for sharing their views and ideas in front of the class often does the trick for bringing them out of distress.

Persisters respond best to the Requestive channel. Soliciting their opinions and asking for data on which they base these opinions assists them in retrieving their knowledge of thoughts and ideas. This helps them focus on factual information and reduces the tendency to push their beliefs on others.

Table 9.3. The Persister in distress

Behaviors	Acts self-righteous (tattles, finds fault with others)
	Expresses rigidity about "my way," "the right way"
	Becomes overly sensitive to negative feedback (needs to be right)
	Uses "you should . . . "
	Is overly suspicious; doesn't trust
	Is sarcastic
	Criticizes others' answers
	Expects perfection of self and others
	Is overly concerned with fairness
	Rolls eyes when others say something "stupid"
	Erases excessively or redoes work to get it perfect
	Becomes upset when others do not believe/respect convictions
	Is stubborn—won't change mind
	Overqualifies comments
	Inserts parenthetical expressions in statements
Needs	Recognition for work
	Conviction
Channel	Requestive
Preventions/ Interventions	Use Requestive channel
	Make positive comments about work
	Give positive public recognition for achievements
	Display work
	Give tangible rewards for work
	Give letter grades
	Select as peer tutor
	Give a leadership role
	Involve in service projects
	Give objectives/rationalizations/relevance for assignments
	Ask about beliefs, opinions, ideas
	Give recognition for beliefs and ideas
	Say "Thank you for sharing your view"
	Say "That's a great idea"
	Provide opportunities for self-evaluations

From Kahler, T. (1982). *Personality pattern inventory validation studies.* Little Rock, AR: Kahler Communications, Inc., and Kahler, T. (1995). *The Process Teaching Seminar.* Little Rock, AR: Kahler Communications, Inc.; adapted by permission.

Setting Up the Classroom for Persisters

Persisters like to give their opinions about various facets of school life, so a suggestion box, advice bulletin board, or column in the school newspaper appeals to them. Persisters appreciate being given the objectives and rationalizations for assignments. When they know the relevance and belief behind tasks in which they participate, they are more likely to buy into them and do their best work. Building in self-evaluations and providing opportunities to evaluate peers also are appealing strategies for Persisters, who need their opinions valued.

DREAMERS

Directions are given, the assignment is distributed, and the lesson has begun. As the teacher glances over at a student he sees that she is looking out the window with the previous assignment still on her desk.

What Do Dreamers in Distress Look Like?

Dreamers in first-degree distress have trouble figuring out what to do (Kahler, 2000). They become easily overwhelmed with the many simultaneous tasks often required in school and have a great deal of difficulty prioritizing multiple assignments. Dreamers are not usually seen with their hands in the air anxious to respond to the question that has just been asked because they need time to process the information and reflect on the answer. In fact, they are sometimes identified as having a processing disability because of the reflection time that they require. They are slow to get out required materials, and although they may not have handed in any of the week's assignments, they frequently have started many of them. Often their desks or notebooks will contain many partly finished assignments.

When Dreamers go into second-degree distress, they will often try to escape either by tuning out or by finding an excuse to physically remove themselves from the classroom. Frequent trips to the bathroom or to the school nurse's or counselor's offices are not un-

common. They may have recurring illnesses that remove them from school. Sustained withdrawal is a clue that Dreamers are not getting their needs met. Sometimes they just tune out. When called on, they don't know what was just asked or what the discussion is about. Often they are still contemplating the answer to the previous question. Teachers need to pay attention to Dreamers in distress so they don't get "lost in the crowd."

How Can We Get Dreamers Out of Distress?

In order to tap into the imaginative and reflective strengths of the Dreamer, solitude is required. This is often difficult to provide in today's classrooms. Finding a space that is away from high-traffic areas, such as a back table or a carrel, might be the solution. Sending them on an errand when they have some time to be alone and to contemplate or letting them go to a corner of the library to complete a specific assignment in an allotted time period can help Dreamers get their need for solitude met. Often, wait time is required for them when responding to a question. Ensuring that the Dreamer understands the directions can often alleviate their distress.

Dreamers respond best to the Directive channel. Cut to the chase with them as soon as you have their attention. Tell them in the simplest form exactly what to do. Give them one or two things to do at a time, and help them prioritize their assignments. Table 9.4

Table 9.4. The Dreamer in distress

Behaviors	Sleeps in class
	Has recurring illnesses
	Escapes: Makes frequent trips to nurse, counselor, bathroom
	Tunes out
	Waits passively
	Doesn't ask questions
	Gets lost in the crowd
	Starts projects and doesn't finish them
	Has difficulty prioritizing multiple assignments
	Does not complete class work or homework
	Does not volunteer
	Daydreams
	Is overly slow to get out materials
	Appears not to hear/understand directions
	Demonstrates sustained withdrawal
	Is nonresponsive
	Shuts down
	Gets left out
Needs	Solitude
	Clear directions; prioritizing
Channel	Directive
Preventions/ Interventions	Use Directive channel
	Give some solitude—carrel, errands, alone time
	Keep out of high traffic areas
	Provide opportunities for individual assignments
	Give clear directions
	Prioritize assignments
	Provide succinct written procedures
	Give only one or two tasks at a time

From Kahler, T. (1982). *Personality pattern inventory validation studies.* Little Rock, AR: Kahler Communications, Inc., and Kahler, T. (1995). *The Process Teaching Seminar.* Little Rock, AR: Kahler Communications, Inc.; adapted by permission.

presents many of the behaviors, needs, channels, and preventions/ interventions that apply to Dreamers in distress.

Setting Up the Classroom for Dreamers

As previously mentioned, Dreamers need to have their assigned seats in low-traffic areas. The corner of the back of the room can often provide the "alone in a crowd" solitude needed, although teachers must keep an eye on Dreamers to ensure that they are on task. Directions should be concise and clear. Teachers facilitate success when they work to ensure that Dreamers have time to contemplate a project or assignment and are provided with a direct description of the required responsibilities. Opportunities to work on assignments alone or perhaps with just one other person appeal to a Dreamer. Dreamer students often need their assignments prioritized for them. Limiting assigned tasks to no more than two or three at a time and writing these or other procedures on a card for them to have in their notebooks or desks are helpful techniques for them. Timelines and organizational structures such as task analysis and graphic organizers will help the Dreamer practice prioritizing and staying on task. Avoid giving Dreamers multiple assignments, big packets of materials, and long-range assignments unless they are broken down into meaningful segments. Teacher follow-up is important to the success of all of these strategies.

REBELS

The class is working on an assignment. The teacher looks around just in time to see a student drop her book on the floor. The student then says in a loud voice to the student next to her, "Hey, why d'ya knock the book off my desk?"

What Do Rebels in Distress Look Like?

It is hard to miss a Rebel who is in first-degree distress. Negative behavior patterns that disrupt the class and make it difficult to teach

soon emerge. The Rebel wants attention and will go to any lengths to get it. Tapping on their desks, falling out of their seats, and making outrageous remarks are just some of the creative ways that Rebels get noticed. They often leave their seats without permission, usually trying to make contact with someone. They may sharpen their pencil repeatedly in order to get attention and perhaps connect with three or four students on the way. They often "play stupid" in class. In a whining and complaining voice they let you know, "This is hard; I don't get it."

When Rebels are in second-degree distress, they blame others. When something goes wrong, they don't take responsibility, even if it is their fault ("He made me do it!"). Selective hearing is evident and "yes, but . . . " is on the tip of their tongue. When frustrated, they will drop out or quit rather than persevere. They adopt an "I'll show you" attitude and often take revenge on their perceived attacker.

How Can We Get Rebels Out of Distress?

Rebels respond to upbeat, positive energy. When teachers notice a Rebel in distress (and they *will* notice!), abruptly changing the activity, giving a high five, or dramatizing a concept can pull the Rebel back into the classroom activity. Sometimes, just stopping to tell a joke or engaging the class in a short physical exercise will bring back the Rebel. The book *The Laughing Classroom* (Loomans & Kolberg, 1995) has a myriad of activities such as the Crazy Handshake or the 60-second "mirth-quake" that can be used to energize Rebels.

Rebels prefer the Emotive channel. Lively communication and high-energy enthusiasm in speaking and dealing with Rebels can keep the classroom a positive place. When teachers experience students' disruptive behaviors, they can change voice tone to an accent, use a different pitch, or talk in a joking manner (not sarcastic) to get Rebels' attention and bring them back to task.

Setting Up the Classroom for Rebels

Rebels are energetic people who like bright colors; loud, lively music; and an environment that invites them to have fun. Therefore, decorating the classroom with brightly colored posters, playing popular music at the start of class and occasionally during class, and greeting them in a friendly, upbeat manner can stimulate them to participate in classroom activities and encourage them to learn. They respond well to lots of movement, hands-on activities, and short spurts of intellectual challenges interspersed with opportunities to use their creativity. Consequently, any learning that can take place through games or multisensory activities will appeal to them.

By incorporating creative assignments such as writing songs, poems, or plays, educators can engage Rebels in some of their favorite pastimes. Determining what Rebels like to do (e.g., singing, acting, writing songs, drawing, painting, playing with puppets or other toys) and finding a way to incorporate these activities into lessons, are sure ways for educators to hook Rebels. Because Rebels need to play first before they have energy to work, starting the class with a joke or riddle that relates to the curriculum can pull them in by meeting their need for playful contact at the beginning of class. Building in a short exercise, a fun activity like the Crazy Handshake (Loomans & Kolberg, 1995), or a short break during which they can leave their seats or socialize, can energize them to focus on tasks they consider more tedious. Greeting them with a high five or a lively comment can help

Table 9.5. The Rebel in distress

Behaviors	Taps on desk
	Falls out of seat
	Drops things
	Sharpens pencil repeatedly
	Gets out of seat without permission
	Plays stupid
	Whines, complains (e.g., "This is hard"; "I don't get it")
	Constantly interrupts to get attention
	Is stubborn, wants own way
	Disrupts the class
	Blames others (e.g., "It's not my fault"; "See what you made me do")
	Plays game of "yes, but . . ."
	Exhibits "I'll show you" attitude
	Knows which buttons to push and pushes them
	Hits, swears, throws things
	Takes revenge—"I'll get you back" attitude
Needs	Playful contact
Channel	Emotive
Preventions/ Interventions	Use Emotive channel
	Provide hands-on activities
	Use games, multisensory activities
	Use computer learning games
	Make demonstrations
	Assign team activities
	Use exclamations
	Use funny voices
	Tell jokes
	Play lively music
	Provide opportunities for dancing
	Use exercises, gross motor activities
	Make use of surprises
	Make use of dramatization
	Provide opportunities for creative activities (e.g., writing songs, poems, plays)

From Kahler, T. (1982). *Personality pattern inventory validation studies.* Little Rock, AR: Kahler Communications, Inc., and Kahler, T. (1995). *The Process Teaching Seminar.* Little Rock, AR: Kahler Communications, Inc.; adapted by permission.

them get their need for playful contact met immediately upon entering the classroom. Rebels can be stubborn and have a tendency to
refuse to do things others order them to do. Punishing them by taking away their recess or making them wait too long to do anything
fun will almost certainly result in their engaging in objectionable
behavior. Table 9.5 presents many of the behaviors, needs, channels,
and preventions/interventions that apply to Rebels in distress.

PROMOTERS

*The teams have been selected, assignments have been given, and
each team is working to solve the problem that was given to them.
Suddenly, one student walks away from his group and refuses to work
with the team, telling them they have to work out a solution themselves
because he is tired of carrying them.*

What Do Promoters in Distress Look Like?

Promoters have a need to "look cool" for their peers and will do anything to save face. In first-degree distress they may get out of their
seats without permission, take a discussion off task, or ask contro-
versial questions. In group activities, they may desert the group,
thereby forcing their teammates to fend for themselves and do all of
the assigned work. Promoters in first-degree distress have a tendency to refuse to do any homework. When this happens, they may
approach their teachers just before the end of the marking period
seeking to make a deal by doing extra work to make up for the work
that was not turned in.

In second-degree distress, Promoters' behavior often appears
manipulative and uncaring. They blame others and manipulate
their classmates—frequently getting them into trouble—whereas
they themselves stay in the background and escape punishment.
They con and make fools of others, ignore or break the rules, lie or
make inflammatory statements, and set up arguments among classmates (e.g., "Why don't you guys duke it out"). Then, they sit back
and watch the fireworks. If Promoters think their teacher is trying to

make them look bad, they may try to turn the tables on the teacher by asking them embarrassing questions, harassing them, or setting up arguments among teachers. When backed into a corner, they will try to twist the situation to embarrass the person they blame for putting them there. This negative drama provides Promotors with action, excitement, and negative recognition.

How Can We Get Promoters Out of Distress?

Promoters are action-oriented individuals who like to live on the edge. They have a lot of energy and need excitement. It is important to channel the energy of Promoters and to ensure that they get the excitement and recognition they need. Providing short-term goals with intermediate rewards for successful performance frequently will help Promoters get their need for action and excitement met positively. Effectively reaching a Promoter often takes creative planning. Sometimes an "antiseptic bounce," which provides an outlet before an outburst, can defuse a potentially explosive situation. Such a technique might include sending the student on an errand or assigning a unique leadership task. Promoters might be given active responsibilities such as passing out materials, operating the projector, recording class notes on the blackboard, presenting group findings to the class, or searching the Web to obtain information on the concept being discussed. It is important to remember that establishing positive rapport with Promoters can be a key ingredient in determining how they behave and perform in the classroom.

Promoters respond best to the Directive channel. Although many students are not comfortable being ordered to do things, this is the most effective way to communicate with Promoters. Therefore, teachers should tell them concisely what they should do, make certain they understand how to do it, and then get out of the way. Letting Promoters clearly know the rules and consequences without setting up a power struggle can eliminate many sources of conflict with them; for example, a teacher could say, "I can hold the radio for you, or you can put it in your backpack."

Setting Up the Classroom for Promoters

The school life of a Promoter must be active and exciting to produce positive energy and satisfaction (Kahler, 2000). Traditional teaching methods such as lecture, whole-class question-and-answer discussions, and lengthy written assignments usually are not effective ways to reach them. Promoters respond much more enthusiastically to competitive games with tangible rewards and prizes. Building in hands-on activities, dramatizations, and ways for Promoters to "look good" will help channel their energies so that they can excel in classroom performance. Promoters enjoy the thrill of making a deal, so they are energized if allowed to bargain. For example, occasionally allowing them to negotiate the parameters of a project or the number of math problems to be done for a particular homework assignment will make them look good to their peers and frequently will motivate them to do their class work. Promoters are natural leaders, and it is in the best interest of teachers and students alike to channel their leadership skills in positive directions. Doing so can be challenging as well as rewarding. When directed in constructive ways such as selecting them as group leaders, putting them in charge of distributing materials, or giving them lead roles in a drama, their energy can be a positive force in the classroom. Because they think

Table 9.6. The Promoter in distress

Behaviors	Gets out of seat without permission
	Needs to save face
	Doesn't complete assignments
	Tries to make deals for extra credit
	Takes over
	Interrupts to ask controversial questions
	Takes discussion off task
	Deserts team members
	Says "you" when meaning "I"
	Gets others into trouble while staying in the background
	Blames others
	Manipulates, uses, and cons others
	Sets up arguments (e.g., "Let's see you guys fight")
	Makes fools of others
	Reverses position unexpectedly
	Breaks or ignores rules
	Makes up or twists situations to others' detriment
	Back stabs
	Persuades others to do negative things
	Makes inaccurate, inflammatory statements
	Sets up negative drama
	Gets physical when outsmarted
Needs	Action
Channel	Directive
Preventions/ Interventions	Use Directive channel
	Provide clear directions
	Move around and gesture while teaching
	Relate content to real world
	Give frequent attention and reinforcement
	Make deals regarding assignments
	Allow to think on feet
	Use competitive games
	Give tangible rewards, prizes
	Make use of surprises (e.g., handshakes, songs)
	Send on errand
	Provide hands-on activities
	Provide opportunities for working with others (with clearly defined rules)
	Provide opportunities for dramatization
	Provide opportunities for demonstrations
	Allow to take on visible leadership role

From Kahler, T. (1982). *Personality pattern inventory validation studies.* Little Rock, AR: Kahler Communications, Inc., and Kahler, T. (1995). *The Process Teaching Seminar.* Little Rock, AR: Kahler Communications, Inc.; adapted by permission.

best on their feet, they should be allowed to stand when they are called on to answer a question. Including activities in lessons that allow them to move around occasionally during a class will keep them interested and motivated. Table 9.6 presents many of the behaviors, needs, channels, and preventions/interventions that apply to Promoters in distress.

CONCLUSION

Symptoms of distress can occur in any classroom at any time throughout the day. With the knowledge of the concepts of Process Communication, teachers can recognize these signs at an early stage and meet the immediate needs of the students who display them. In addition, they can use this knowledge to ensure that their own needs are met. By using the techniques described previously, teachers can prevent or intervene quickly to reduce student anxiety. When teachers can discern the personality types of their students and engage them in activities to get their needs met, challenging situations can become opportunities to make significant positive contributions to the class. The keys to doing this are being able to identify the personality type of each student and being able to implement strategies to meet their individual needs. A classroom in which the teacher and the students get their needs met is a happy and productive place for everyone!

A POUND OF CURE

ENGAGING ALL STUDENTS IN THE LEARNING PROCESS

CHAPTER 10

Chapter 9 discusses the various degrees of stress that students experience throughout the school day. Students manifest their distress in a variety of ways depending on personality type, and the resulting behaviors can be disruptive to the learning process.

As teachers become more accountable for the academic success of a diverse student population, they need tools that will help them engage students more fully in the learning process so that all students can reach their full potential. The concepts of PCM provide teachers with a wider variety of techniques to meet the needs of students in today's heterogeneous classrooms. Four educational tools have been created that complement the use of PCM in the school setting. We examine each of these in depth and look at how each can be incorporated into the context of planning for the success of all students. The four tools are

1. *Lesson Planning Questions:* six basic questions that teachers can ask themselves while they are planning a lesson or unit that will assist them in reaching the six types of students through their instruction

2. *Student Intervention Plan (SIP):* helps the educators who work with a particular student to identify the student's personality profile and then develop interventions based on the student's specific needs

3. *Functional Behavioral Assessment (FBA):* widely used in special education to determine the function of undesirable behaviors exhibited by students and to develop a successful intervention plan (The SIP and FBA are especially effective with students whose distress is causing them to engage in disruptive and destructive behaviors.)

4. *100+ Process Communication Ways to Praise a Child:* handy table that gives teachers a quick way to give feedback to their students that incorporates individual personality preferences. Although many lists of positive comments for teachers to make to students exist, this is the first one that has been developed specifically for use with the six personality types as identified by PCM.

LESSON-PLANNING QUESTIONS

Educators who have been trained to use PCM have found success in reaching all six types of learners. As we have seen from previous chapters, most teachers' strengths center around the characteristics and energy found in Persisters; Workaholics; and, in the case of many elementary school teachers, Reactors. Because educators tend to use the teaching styles with which they are most comfortable, most classrooms abound in lecture, reading, writing, and question–answer discussions. Students with histories of school difficulties, both behavioral and academic, however, are often not reached when materials are presented based only on the teacher's preferences for learning. As a result, they may be referred for special education.

The planning stage of a lesson or unit is, then, the place for teachers to ask themselves the six questions that can ensure that the needs of all six types of students are being met (see Figure 10.1). Reactors need personal recognition, whereas Workaholics and Persisters need recognition for work. In addition, Workaholics benefit from being given a time structure, whereas, Persisters need tasks to be meaningful. Dreamers will need some reflection/processing time as well as personal space. If the task can be perceived as fun it will appeal to the Rebel, and if it incorporates some action Promoters will respond positively. When all of these views are considered in the teacher's plans, success for each type of student is more probable, and disruptions are less likely to occur.

Figure 10.2 shows activities planned for a math lesson that answer the questions posed in Figure 10.1 so that the needs of all six types of students are met. The math lesson for the day is to review addition and subtraction word problems. Students work with partners to make up a problem and act it out. The other students have to figure out whether it is an addition or a subtraction problem and solve the equation. Points are given to each pair that is able to identify the operation and solve the problem correctly. If students stay on task, they get 5 minutes of free time at the end of the lesson.

An educator can meet many of the Reactors' needs informally by making a personal comment to these students as they are working in their groups. Reactors also enjoy working with a partner because group membership is important to them. Workaholics respond

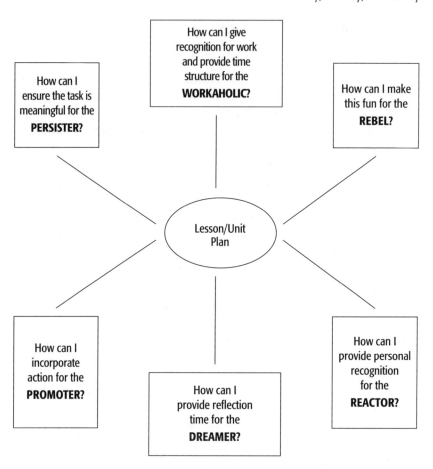

Figure 10.1. Process Communication Model lesson/unit plan questions.

to knowing when the lesson begins and ends. They also enjoy the thought processes of identifying the math operations and solving the problems. Because the problems apply to real-life situations, Persisters understand the purpose of the assignment. Acting out the problems appeals to both Rebels and Promoters—it is fun and they get to be center stage. Giving points and rewards for correct answers also keeps the Promoters interested. Dreamers can be kept on task and can have more opportunities to share their ideas when working with only one other person. They look forward to the free time at the end for some solitude.

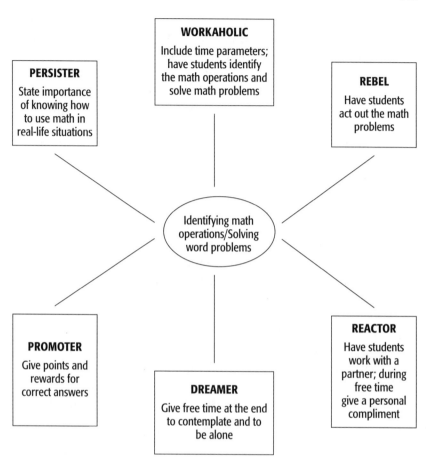

Figure 10.2. Process Communication Model planning schema for math lesson.

One elementary school special education teacher in Maryland incorporates the lesson planning questions in the following way: She establishes an immediate connection with each of her students as they enter the room by greeting them by name and with a smile. She takes a few seconds to connect with them on a personal level with comments such as, "Joey, you got new glasses!" "It's good to see you, Lakisha, we missed you yesterday." "Juan, I heard your mother was in the hospital—how is she doing?" The Reactors immediately know that she cares personally about them. She might also give a high five and an enthusiastic comment to her Rebel students.

She then distributes a list of activities similar to the one in Figure 10.3. This immediately appeals to the Workaholic because it provides structure and organization for the assignments. The first thing she asks the students to do is to look at the clothes on the line at the top and pick the craziest (appeals to Rebels) or the one they like best (appeals to Reactors) and color it with the array of colored pens she has provided. This activity is motivating for Promoters, Rebels, and Reactors as they each like to put their personal, creative mark on the pictures. The students then read the plans together while putting their fingers on each of the pictures to keep their place. This gives Rebels and Promoters kinesthetic involvement and helps the Dreamers stay on task. Her Workaholic students enjoy helping her read the assignments. As the teacher reviews the objectives, the significance of the assignments becomes evident to the Persisters. The teacher explains that the guided reading will be done individually, and she will come around and read with each student. This is a relief to the Dreamers who know they will get some "alone" time.

One high school chemistry teacher uses the lesson planning questions to prepare all of her lessons. To help students understand the elements, she puts a list of all of the elements on the bulletin board, and each student signs up for his or her "favorite element." She then hands out a schedule telling when each part of the assignment is due. The students research the element and prepare a 1-minute presentation to explain its properties and important uses. Using the information they have learned, they make a costume representing their element, which they wear when making the presentation. In subsequent lessons and in their labs, they may get to do experiments with their element. The Workaholic and Persister students enjoy doing the research. The Workaholic students are happy to learn when each part of the assignment is due because this allows them to plan their time. The Persisters are able to form an opinion about the importance of their element. Reactors enjoy the opportunity to describe how they feel being that element. The Dreamer students find imaginative ways to present the material, for example by writing a poem about it. They also appreciate being able to work alone doing the assignment. The Rebel students have fun and are able to use their creativity in making their costumes. They like having an opportunity to move about and to present in front of the class. The Promoter students also have an opportunity to move around and are

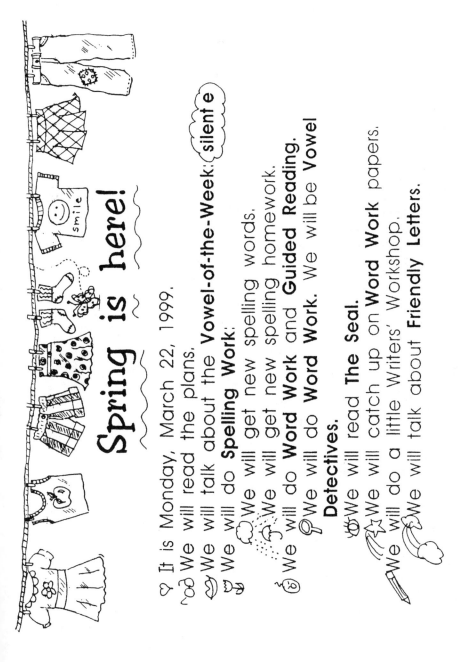

Spring is here!

♡ It is Monday, March 22, 1999.

We will read the plans.

We will talk about the **Vowel-of-the-Week:** silent e

We will do **Spelling Work:**

We will get new spelling words.

We will get new spelling homework.

We will do **Word Work** and **Guided Reading.**

We will do **Word Work.** We will be Vowel **Detectives.**

We will read **The Seal.**

We will catch up on **Word Work** papers.

We will do a little Writers' Workshop.

We will talk about **Friendly Letters.**

Figure 10.3. Sample handout showing list of classroom activities. (From Rosen, M.D., & Weinstock, V.F. [1999]. Class handout from Montgomery County Public Schools, MD; reprinted by permission.)

147

right at home being center stage. In subsequent lessons and labs involving their elements, students work in pairs and in small groups doing the assignments. The Reactors enjoy the social aspects of the group activities. The Rebels and Promoters enjoy the hands-on nature of the labs and the ability to work on their feet and move around. The Workaholics and Persisters enjoy doing the research and working with a partner. The Dreamers usually do not actively participate in the small groups, but in the labs they can work with a partner or alone.

Another teacher, who works with adolescents with emotional disabilities, decided that instead of giving his high school students a list of review questions to study for the American government test, he would put the questions in the form of a game and play Jeopardy! with them. He assigns dollar values to the questions based on difficulty and puts them in pockets on a chart that has ranges from $50 to $500. The class is divided into teams. Members from each team take turns coming up to the chart and selecting a question to answer. After conferring with their teammates, they give an oral answer to the question. They get point tickets for each correct answer. If one team is not able to answer the question, the other team has a chance. As the students come up to the chart to pick their questions and the teams figure out the answers together, it is evident that all students are involved in the academic activity. This is much preferred over the typical behaviors these students display in times of stress, including making derogatory comments to each other, questioning the teacher's authority, making noises, asking to leave the room, and engaging in other off-task behaviors.

Promoters especially like the risk-taking and competition factors involved in this game. Reactors and Rebels like working with their peers, and there are smiles all around at the cheers from their classmates when they get points for their team. Workaholics and Persisters respond to the structure of the game format (rules) and are able to get recognition for their knowledge (the $500 questions). Dreamers know that if they can't think of an answer right away, they may confer with teammates. At the end of the game, students are rewarded with snacks and 5 minutes of free time. Some students use their free time to socialize, some for further study, some to work or play at the computer, and some just to get a bit of alone time. The teacher reported that students spent more time engaged with the curriculum during this activity than in his more traditional teaching formats because of the lack of distracting student behaviors. Furthermore, students who have completed this activity usually perform better on the test than they had on past assessments.

Teachers have also found that if they introduce their lessons with a "battery charge," a way for students of each personality type to get their needs met, they tend to pay more attention. Even if they can't "play" or have time alone or "do something" right away, they tend to tune in better because they know "there will be something in this for me!" Following are some lesson/unit introductions designed by teachers specifically to appeal to each of the six types of learners in their classrooms.

Introducing the Lesson/Unit

This lesson was done with a high school special education English class studying Romeo and Juliet.

Today, we prepare to go to a masque ball at the home of Lord Capulet. To prepare ourselves for the masque, we will read Act I, Scene V of *Romeo and Juliet* following along with the CD. Then from our FYI (direction) sheets, we'll learn how to make a mask for the party. Remember, Lord Capulet is a prominent, wealthy member of Verona, and we want to impress him with our mask. Listen carefully to the descriptions of the masque ball in the reading, remembering the meaning that Elizabethans ascribed to certain colors, metals, and materials. Stations with art supplies are set up around the room for you to use, or you can use materials you have brought with you. When your mask is complete, write a paragraph citing the significance of the mask and materials that you chose. The assignment is worth a total of 25 points. We will display our masks on our Communications Bulletin Board when they are completed.

One student in the class had not done any writing assignments for the entire year. For this assignment, he completed the mask and wrote a short paragraph!

This next unit was done in a middle school science class that contained many students with special needs. The teacher got the students' attention by blowing an imaginary horn.

"OK, everybody! You know that we have been talking, reading, and learning about recycling. Today we are going to put all our hard work into action and make our own recycled paper. First, we are going to get into teams. Each team will have 2 minutes to make trash out of the paper I've given them and put it in the trash can with that team's color on it. Then I'm going to give a short demonstration on how to make recycled paper and go over the step-by-step directions. After that, each student will be given the responsibility of following one step in the directions, and with help from our teammates, *voilà,* the paper is recycled! It will have to dry overnight, and tomorrow our teams will decorate the beautiful creations they have made from trash. So tonight, think about how you would like to decorate your creations."

———————————

An elementary teacher introduced a persuasive writing lesson to her class in the following way:

"Today, we will not only write but also design a product—the 'Sleek Sneak!' We're going to have lots of fun! Here is the story: I am a sneaker manufacturer. I am looking for a new and different sneaker. First, your job will be to design a sneaker with the items I have set up here on the table (cut-out of a sneaker, markers, glitter, glue, stars, dots, beads, material). Then, you will write about your sneaker and give me your opinion as to why I should manufacture your Sleek Sneak. Work anywhere in the room you would like. No idea is wrong—all are accepted! You will have 40 minutes to work on your sneaker this morning and 40 minutes to work on your written presentation this afternoon. A prize will be awarded for the sneakers that are selected to be manufactured, but the 'manufacturer' has promised a surprise for everyone who participates. Tomorrow, all of the 'Sleek Sneaks' will 'walk the walls' to the bulletin board where the winners will be displayed."

When teachers capitalize on their natural resourcefulness and creativity, lessons and units that appeal to each of the six personality types can be designed to help students stay on task and learn as much as possible in each class. The six lesson planning questions in Figure 10.1 have also been adapted by administrators when conducting meetings with their staff or with parents.

One principal opened her first Parent–Teacher Association meeting of the year as follows:

"Good evening, parents! Thank you so much for giving up your time and the comfort of your homes to attend the PTA meeting this evening. Wow! It's exciting to see so many of you here! It's clear that those of you who are here model your belief in the important role parents play in the school life of children. We have some refreshments to help make it comfortable and cozy. Tonight we have planned a variety of exciting ways to share some important information. We think it will also be fun and helpful when you have had the opportunity to meet new faces in our school community. So let's get started so we can be finished at the scheduled time of 8:30.

One administrator wanted his staff to examine test data of the students in his school. After giving his staff time to review the school's standardized test results, he structured the meeting in the following way:

"Now that your grade-level teams have had a chance to examine the test data for our school, I have posted six questions on charts around the room. Take some time to walk around and read each question. After you have read the questions, think of the one question you would feel most comfortable responding to. When your group seems to be together, please begin answering the question and writing your ideas on the chart. You will have 45 minutes to complete this activity. Please make sure that each group has a recorder, a spokesperson, and the needed supplies before you begin. Here are the questions:

1. Based on the test data, what do you **think** should be our academic goals for this year?

2. What internal supports do you **feel** we have that will allow us to achieve academic success on the tests?

3. What external challenges do you **believe** we face that impede our academic achievement on these tests?

4. What **creative** supports should we explore that might result in drastic academic growth as measured by these assessments?

5. What action could we **contemplate** to help our students improve on these tests?

6. What types of **fun and exciting** celebrations would you suggest we consider to celebrate our current success on these tests?

The administrator noted that the people on his staff gravitated to the question that best matched their personality type. After the allotted 45 minutes, each group reported back to the whole group. The responses were used to formulate the school plan for student improvement on standardized tests.

Knowledge of the six personality types can help all educators reach not only their students but also many more of their staff and community members.

STUDENT INTERVENTION PLANS

Although most teachers are successful with most of their students, there are students in almost every classroom whose behavior bewilders and frustrates their teachers. These students could be any of the six personality types and could be in general education classes, special education classes, or alternative education classes. To help teachers accurately assess the reasons for these behaviors and to identify successful strategies to use with these students, Smith and Pauley (1999) developed the Student Intervention Plan (SIP) (see Figure 10.4a). This form may be helpful for students who continually disrupt the class, tend to tune out, have frequent absences, cry, can't sit still, constantly challenge the teacher, or otherwise disrupt their own and others' learning.

The SIP can be completed by an individual teacher or by a team of teachers who work with a particular student. Strengths and behavioral weaknesses are identified. Educators usually have no trouble identifying the personality type! After the personality structure of the student is constructed, psychological needs, channels of communication, and distress behaviors are noted. One target behavior at a time is then selected, and the teacher or team members brainstorm intervention strategies based on their knowledge of needs, channels, and distress behaviors exhibited on an Intervention Strategy Log (see Figure 10.4b). The strategies are then implemented, and the success of the strategies is noted. A number of strategies can be tried and then assessed for success. Sometimes the strategies are so simple; it is surprising they can have such a big impact!

One teacher was worried about a fifth-grade boy in her class, Eric, who demonstrated the distress behaviors of crying, getting sick, and having to leave the room—all of

Student _____ Grade _____

Strengths	Behavioral weaknesses	Personality structure	Psychological needs	Channel	Distress behaviors
		6.			
		5.			
		4.			
		3.			
		2.			
		1.			

Figure 10.4a. Blank Student Intervention Plan (SIP) form, Part I. (From Smith, K.D., & Pauley, J.F. [1999, April]. *What to do about Bernie: Teaching and reaching the hard-to-reach student.* Paper presented at the national conference of the Council for Exceptional Children, Charlotte, NC.; reprinted by permission.)

Problem being addressed	Strategies used	Success of strategies

Figure 10.4b. Blank Student Intervention Plan (SIP) form, Part II, Intervention Strategy Log. (From Smith, K.D., & Pauley, J.F. [1999, April]. *What to do about Bernie: Teaching and reaching the hard-to-reach student.* Paper presented at the national conference of the Council for Exceptional Children, Charlotte, NC.; reprinted by permission.)

which were naturally detracting from his school progress. She identified him as a Reactor (see Figure 10.5a). After the teacher identified his type, his needs, and his preferred channel, she decided to meet and greet him with a warm word and smile every morning (see Figure 10.5b). The result of this almost effortless intervention was dramatic—Eric's attendance improved, there was a reduction in crying, and he was sick less often—all of which made him much more available for learning! Other teachers have had success with students who

Student Eric   Grade 5

Strengths	Behavioral weaknesses	Personality structure	Psychological needs	Channel	Distress behaviors
Good reader

Understands new concepts readily

Loving

Excellent ideas in discussions | Poor self-image

Quick to say he doesn't understand

Short attention span | 6. Workaholic

5. Persister

4. Promoter

3. Rebel

2. Dreamer

1. Reactor | Recognition of person

Sense of belonging

Clear directions

Help with priorities | Nurturative | Self-denigrates
Cries
Gets sick |

Figure 10.5a. Sample Student Intervention Plan (SIP), Part I, for Eric, a Reactor.

Problem being addressed	Strategies used	Success of strategies
Poor self-image	Smiled directly at student and told how glad she was to see him as he entered the room in the morning	Stopped getting sick during the day

Figure 10.5b. Sample Intervention Strategy Log, Part II, for Eric, a Reactor.

Student Jonté   Grade 7

Strengths	Behavioral weaknesses	Personality structure	Psychological needs	Channel	Distress behaviors
Regular attendance	Horseplay/ physical aggression	6. Reactor	Playful contact	Emotive	Takes revenge
		5. Workaholic	Spontaneity	(Avoid Directive)	Plays rough
Creative Writing	Bullying other students	4. Dreamer	Creativity		Blames others
Strong math skills		3. Persister			Quits
	Not following directions	2. Promoter			Taps
	Shows no remorse	1. Rebel			

Figure 10.6a.   Sample Student Intervention Plan (SIP), Part I, for Jonté, a Rebel.

Problem being addressed	Strategies used	Success of strategies
Horse play/physical aggression during class and transitions	Relocation in classroom	Didn't do well; started making noise, teasing and interfering with instruction
	Proximity control–redirected– appealed to values	Worked well sometimes; still teasing and making noise
	Used creative writing as a reward–15 minutes per class	Worked well sometimes; still out of location and disturbing other students
	Greeted at the door (contact need) and gave leadership roles in the classroom	Almost always had a good day and concentrated on tasks
	Played basketball before school with friends to decrease excessive energy and get playful contact	Behavior improved greatly

Figure 10.6b.   Sample Intervention Strategy Log, Part II, for Jonté, a Rebel.

Strengths	Behavioral weaknesses	Personality structure	Psychological needs	Channel	Distress behaviors
Attends school regularly

Has friends

Respectful to all adults in school | Unorganized

Does not pay attention in class

Does not participate in class

Completes no classwork or homework | 6. Workaholic

5. Persister

4. Rebel

3. Promoter

2. Reactor

1. Dreamer | Solitude

Clear directions | Directive | Leaves class whenever possible

Difficulty prioritizing multiple assignments

Does not volunteer

Slow to get out materials

Starts projects and doesn't finish them

Tunes out

Passively waits |

Figure 10.7a. Sample Student Intervention Plan (SIP), Part I, for Stan, a Dreamer.

Problem being addressed	Strategies used	Success of strategies
Not completing any school-work or homework	Discussed failing grades with student and parent	No change
	Moved seat to front with three other students	No change
	Moved seat next to adult with one other student	Participated more in class and asked questions. Did some homework
	Recognized student for accomplishments on bulletin board and privately by one adult	Stayed on task for given assignment and finished when given encouragement and then left alone

Figure 10.7b. Sample Intervention Strategy Log, Part II, for Stan, a Dreamer.

Student Jamie _____   Grade 2 _____

Strengths	Behavioral weaknesses	Personality structure	Psychological needs	Channel	Distress behaviors
Math facts

Basic reading skills

Likes to color and draw

Likes responsibility jobs

Interested in animals, dinosaurs

Enjoys books and pictures | Calls out, interrupts

Physical aggression

Shows no remorse

Hyperactive, impulsive

Short attention span

Difficulty staying in own space

Argues | 6. Workaholic

5. Dreamer

4. Persister

3. Reactor

2. Promoter

1. Rebel | Playful contact

Fun | Emotive | Interrupting

Talking loudly

"I don't know what do do"

Arguing

Physical aggression

Blames others

Difficulty staying in own space |

Figure 10.8a.   Sample Student Intervention Plan (SIP), Part I, for Jamie, a Rebel.

Problem being addressed	Strategies used	Success of strategies
Calling out, interrupting during whole group instruction	Proximity control

Redirected using agreed upon signal

Made contract—see if he can "beat" his baseline number

Gave reward of intermittent playing a game for 3-minute intervals | Baseline of call-outs reduced from 26 times in a 30-minute period to 3 times in a 30-minute period |

Figure 10.8b.   Student Intervention Strategy Log, Part II, for Jamie, a Rebel.

are aggressive (see Figure 10.6a and b), who tune out (see Figure 10.7a and b), and who call out excessively (see Figure 10.8a and b).

The SIP can be an especially helpful tool in developing goals and objectives for students' individualized education programs (IEPs). For instance, Jonté, a Rebel described in Figure 10.6a, has an IEP for emotional disabilities. One of his goals as identified on the SIP is to reduce aggression and inappropriate play during class and transitions. Strategies are delineated on his intervention strategy log (Figure 10.6b), and the success of the strategies can be indicated by anecdotal or numerical records.

Stan, who is a Dreamer (Figure 10.7a), has a learning disability. The problem being addressed on his SIP is completion of schoolwork and homework. This is also a goal on his IEP. Successful (as well as unsuccessful) strategies for assisting Stan with accomplishing this goal are evident on his intervention strategy log (Figure 10.7b) and can be shared with all of his teachers.

The SIP is an extremely useful tool because it helps pinpoint interventions that work for specific types instead of using generic interventions such as behavior contracts that work for some students but not for others. Some teachers have found it useful to implement the SIP with the whole class so that they have strategies already thought out for each student. The intervention can be tailored to fit the specific needs and personality type of the individual student. For instance, one team decided to use a behavior contract with a second-grade student, Jamie, who, because of his high Rebel/Promoter energy, was repeatedly calling out without raising his hand (Figure 10.8a). The key to the success of his contract was a "contest." The student tried to beat his own scores by reducing the number of call-outs per day (which met his Promoter need for excitement/competition), and his reward consisted of being allowed to play with puppets at intermittent times during the day (met his Rebel need for fun). His behavior dramatically improved from 26 call-outs in a 30-minute period to 3 call-outs in a 30-minute period in just 3 weeks (Figure 10.8b)!

FUNCTIONAL BEHAVIORAL ASSESSMENTS

FBAs are used extensively with special education students to help determine the most appropriate interventions for those who are experiencing behavior problems. The process is often extended to incorporate any student who might be displaying negative or unacceptable behaviors in school.

The FBA identifies the relationship between environmental events and the manifestation of a particular behavior. It is based on the premise that problem behavior results from unmet needs. The purpose of an FBA is to assess the behavior in question to determine the function, purpose, or need that it serves for the student and then to develop a plan that helps the student get that need met in an appropriate manner. Students who exhibit challenging behaviors do so for a variety of reasons. As Carpenter, Musy, and King-Sears told us, "Many inappropriate behaviors are communicative in nature in that they serve to fulfill students' needs" (1997, p. 345).

The FBA usually is conducted by a team of educators (see Figure 10.9). The team first identifies the behavior(s) that is (are) getting the student into trouble. This should be done in as measurable terms as possible. "The student is overactive" does not specify in measurable terms what is really going on. "The student is out of her seat 12 times in a 20-minute period," however, is much more specific and provides educators and others a measurable behavior with which to work.

The next step is to gather data through a variety of sources. A thorough record review is done to see if that sheds some light on possible causes and to ascertain patterns of behavior; observations of the

Date/time	Antecedent	Behavior	Consequence/function
	What happened immediately before the problem behavior (setting and trigger event)?	Exactly what did you observe the student doing in measurable terms?	What happened immediately after the problem behavior? What need did it meet?

Figure 10.9. Blank functional behavioral assessment (FBA) form.

Table 10.1. Antecedent, behavior, and consequence (ABC) chart for Shawn

Antecedent	Behavior	Consequence
Teacher gives assignment	Shawn draws	Shawn doesn't do the work
Teacher gives a reminder	Shawn whines	Shawn doesn't do the work
Teacher becomes firm	Shawn becomes defiant; calls the teacher a name	Shawn gets attention from his classmates; doesn't do the work
Teacher asks him to leave the class	Shawn leaves class	Shawn wins the power struggle; doesn't do the work

student are done to collect specific behavioral data; and interviews are conducted with the parent, student, and/or teachers.

Several observations of student behavior are conducted to examine the antecedent, behavior, and consequence (ABC) of the student's problematic action. The observer watches for the targeted action (behavior) and then determines what took place right before this action (antecedent). What then occurs as a result of the student's behavior is noted (consequence). As the relationship between what occurred in the student's environment that triggered the behavior and the specific behavior are determined, the antecedent can be altered to promote a replacement behavior that can serve the same purpose or get the same need met.

For example, Shawn might be refusing to do any written work. The observer notices that when the social studies teacher assigns the students to answer the questions at the end of the chapter, Shawn gets out a piece of paper and draws pictures. When the teacher tells him to get to work, he whines and says it's too hard. When she continues to prod him to start his work, he becomes defiant and says he is not going to do it. The teacher tells him that if he's not going to work in her class he can just go to the office. Shawn slams out of the classroom, calling the teacher a name. Let's examine this situation in the light of ABC, as shown in Table 10.1.

Although the teacher's goal was to get Shawn to do his assignment, Shawn succeeded in manipulating the situation so that he not only got out of doing the work but also got the attention of his classmates and won a power struggle with the teacher.

The team then looks at these data and hypothesizes about the causes of the behavior, which they list in writing (see Table 10.2). Why doesn't Shawn do his work? Is the work too difficult or too easy for him? Does he need some type of recognition or reassurance from the teacher? Is he trying to look "cool" in front of his friends? Is he trying to generate a little excitement? The team members try to determine why the student engages in this particular behavior and what need is not being met.

In this case, the team determines that, given Shawn's low reading level, he probably would have a lot of difficulty reading the chapter and answering the questions. Not wanting to risk anyone finding this out, he refuses to even attempt the assignment.

When all of the data are analyzed by the team, a positive behavioral support plan is developed. This plan includes changing the antecedent in an attempt to reduce the occurrence of the negative behavior. Changes might include giving the student the option of reading and answering the questions with a partner, listening to a recording of the chapter and illustrating the answers to the questions, or providing individual instruction with Shawn and other students who are having the same types of reading difficulties. When the antecedent is manipulated, the behavior often will change.

Table 10.2.   Evaluating possible reasons behind behaviors

The intent or purpose of the behavior could be for a variety of reasons, including

- To learn at an appropriate level of instruction (current instruction may be too high or too low)
- To escape or avoid a frustrating task or event
- To gain or avoid attention
- To seek or reject power or control
- To seek or reject tangible reinforcement
- To seek or avoid sensory stimulation
- To obtain a preferred task
- To seek some excitement or fun
- To seek solitude

Table 10.3. Another example of an antecedent, behavior, and consequence (ABC) chart

Antecedent	Behavior	Consequence
Teacher assigns homework orally at the end of class.	Student rarely brings homework to class.	Student has to stay in at lunch and complete homework assignment.

The purpose of the intervention is to identify a change in strategy, technique, or teacher behavior that helps the student get his or her needs met in a more positive way. *It is imperative at this point to know the student's personality type.* If Shawn is a Workaholic and doesn't want his classmates to know that he is having difficulty with the work, his motivation for not wanting to start the assignment might be very different than if he is a Reactor who feels that the teacher doesn't like him or a Promoter who is bored and wants to stir up some action. If Shawn is a Dreamer, he may benefit the most by listening to the chapter on tape. If he is a Rebel, he would probably respond well to working in a group and illustrating the answers. Once his personality type and corresponding needs are identified, the most appropriate intervention can be selected. The main point to remember is to find alternative behaviors that serve the same function (i.e., meet the same need) as the questionable behavior. Therefore, knowing the personality type of the student can help us quickly determine the need that is not being met.

Table 10.3 examines another behavior in order to help identify the need that is not being met and to devise some appropriate interventions for a student. Again, it is crucial to determine the personality type of the student in order to plan an effective intervention. Table 10.4 examines the consequence of this particular behavior based on the motivations of each personality type and the need(s) associated with that type. Antecedents are changed to solicit alternative behaviors.

The purpose of the FBA is to ensure that the student's needs are being met in an acceptable fashion. The need of a Dreamer is to have some solitude, whereas a Rebel needs to have playful contact. The way in which the teacher delivers the materials and interacts with students can be a key factor—if an assignment is given in the Emo-

Table 10.4. Motivations and interventions

Personality type	Psychological needs being met	Motivation for behavior	Appropriate intervention (antecedent) to promote behavior change
Reactor	Recognition of person	Gets to stay in at lunch with teacher and have more personal time	Greet student at door and ask a personal question; ask student to write homework assignment on board to help everyone.
Workaholic	Recognition for work, time structure	Receives extra help needed without looking stupid in front of peers	Make sure that work is on student's level; give praise for work whenever possible; praise effort; make sure student writes down assignment; give individual help when possible.
Persister	Conviction	Gets time to argue with teacher about the fairness of the assignment	Ask student's opinion whenever possible; praise commitment of student when homework is turned in; discuss importance of responsibility.
Dreamer	Solitude, structure	Receives assignment individually from teacher; can work on assignment alone with no distractions	Give student solitude during class time; check student's assignment book to see that assignment is written down; communicate with parent to help structure assignments and give student privacy at home.
Rebel	Playful contact	Gets to be the center of attention for the teacher; gets the teacher's undivided attention	Give one-on-one attention in a playful manner in class; let student announce the homework to the class.
Promoter	Incidence, excitement	Gets to maintain cool persona in front of peers; provides opportunity to "make a deal" with teacher about homework	Have student check to see if everyone writes down the homework assignment. At the beginning of next class, have student spot check who did the homework.

164

tive channel with an upbeat voice and a secret signal, that may be all that is necessary to hook in a Rebel. On the other hand, if a Workaholic is having difficulty with the material, a teacher's best response may be to employ a method for having the student achieve academic success and praise the student for small segments of correct work.

The FBA interfaces well with the SIP. The most effective interventions for students demonstrating troubling behaviors are those that use a combination of the two. As the target behavior is identified and needs based on personality type are examined, intervention strategies can be developed that are tailored to meeting the specific need(s) of that personality type. Using this approach will most likely result in a change to more positive student behavior.

100+ PROCESS COMMUNICATION WAYS TO PRAISE A CHILD

Feedback is one of the most important aspects of teaching. Thus, when we experience an intervention that has been successful for one student, we put it in our repertoire in hopes that it will work with all students. Students need our commendations and positive recog-

Reactors

(Nurturative tone)
You're special
Beautiful
You're incredible
You're fantastic
How smart
You're beautiful
I like you
Beautiful work
Marvelous
Terrific
You're important
You're sensational
What a good listener
You care
Beautiful sharing
You're important
You mean a lot to me
You brighten my day
You're a joy
You're a treasure
You're wonderful
You're the best
You're a good friend
You're really something

Workaholics

(Matter-of-fact tone)
Outstanding
Excellent
Great work
Well done
Nice work
Fantastic job
Super work
Super job
Fantastic job
Exceptional performance
You are responsible
What a good listener
That's correct
A+ job
That's the best
You did a lot of work
  today
You're doing a fine job
Keep up the good work
Good thinking
Good idea

Promoters

(Upbeat tone)
Neat!
Well done
Remarkable
Looking good
You're on top of it
Now you're flying!
You're catching on
Bravo!
You're fantastic
You're on target!
You're on your way!
Nothing can stop you now!
You're a winner!
You're spectacular!
Great discovery!
You've discovered the
  secret!
You are exciting
Awesome!
Way to wrap it up
You make it look so easy
I've never seen anyone do
  it better
Nothing can stop you now
That was a first-class idea
Right on!

Dreamers

(Low-key, direct tone)
Good
Now you've got it
You're on target
Nothing can stop you now
You figured it out
You're a real trooper
That's correct
I knew you could do it
You're on the right track
Now you have it
You're really concentrating
You did that very well
Perfect
Great idea
Imaginative idea
Great insights

Rebels

(Upbeat tone)
Wow!
Way to go!
Excellent!
I knew you could do it!
Fantastic!
Superstar!
Looking good!
Now you're flying
Now you've got it!
You're incredible!
Hurray for you!
That's amazing!
Dynamite!
You're unique
You're A-OK!
Tremendous!
You're a winner!
Remarkable!
Spectacular!
Hip, hip, hurray!
Right on
Creative job!
You are exciting!
What an imagination!
Awesome!
You've really got your brain in gear
How did you think of that?
You make my job so much fun!
You sure fooled me!

Persisters

(Matter-of-fact tone)
I'm proud of you
What's your opinion?
Great idea
You make meaningful contributions
Good for you
Great discovery
Phenomenal
Creative job
Exceptional performance
What a good listener
A+ job
I trust you
That's exactly right
Good thinking
You're very good at that
I value your ideas

Figure 10.10. 100+ Process Communication ways to praise a child.

nition. Many teachers who are making an effort to give more positive feedback keep a list of the various comments they make to their
students to give them this recognition. When they can identify the
personality type of the student who needs some specific attention,
however, they are able to make more appropriate interventions. Figure 10.10 lists the types of things to say to encourage students based
on their personality type. For example, "Good job" is the perfect
statement to make to a Workaholic who needs recognition for work
but has little meaning to a Reactor or a Rebel and may in fact, have
a negative impact. "I'm glad you're here" shows a Reactor that your
relationship isn't dependent on what he or she produces. "Way to go!"
tells a Rebel that fun as well as the job is important to you. Students
also respond positively to receiving written comments on their
papers. For instance, when a student has worked hard on rewriting
an essay, a comment such as "This is very insightful—I'd really like
you to share it with the class" would appeal to several different personality types. All would appreciate the comment about the work
being insightful; Rebels, Promoters, Workaholics, and Persisters
would especially enjoy sharing their work with the class. Keeping
this chart close when grading papers or projects can help target written feedback so that students' needs continue to be met.

CONCLUSION

It is essential for all of us to get our needs met. When students are
not able to get their needs met positively at school they distract others, tune out, worry, argue, and misbehave. Obviously, not much
learning can take place when students are engaged in these types of
behaviors. However, "Learners who feel that their needs are being
met in the classroom seldom cause discipline problems because interfering with something that is meeting a need is contrary to their self-
interest" (Savage, 1991, p. 39). If we look back at Figures 1.4 and 1.5
in Chapter 1, we can see the basic needs and preferred channels of
communication identified for each personality type. Teachers who
make an effort to address these needs specifically and to use a variety of communication channels, especially with those students who
are keeping themselves from learning by displaying disruptive behav-

iors in the classroom, can help put them in a state in which they are ready to learn.

Using the four tools of Lesson Planning Questions, SIPs, FBAs, and 100+ Process Communication Ways to Praise a Child can help teachers pinpoint specific strategies to use with their students so that maximum learning with minimum disruption can take place in their classrooms. These tools help teachers meet the needs of their students and aid them in using the concepts of PCM in their planning, teaching, and classroom management.

KEEPING TEACHERS OUT OF DISTRESS

CHAPTER 11

In Chapter 9 we examined what students who do not get their needs met will do when in distress, and we explored the ways in which educators can intervene to head off these negative behaviors. In the course of a school day, however, students are not the only ones who experience pressure and stress. Even the best teachers may periodically find themselves in a distressed state. This chapter shows some of the typical behaviors that teachers of each personality type demonstrate when they are in distress. It also explores the reasons for their distress and suggests ways they can reduce their stress level. As teachers of each type describe their distress behaviors, they demonstrate warning signs that indicate the importance of getting their specific motivational needs met positively.

TEACHER STRESSORS

In a survey conducted with teachers at the elementary and secondary levels, the authors found that educators consistently noted the following as primary sources of stress (Bradley, Pauley, & Pauley, 2001):

1. *Assessment and accountability:* More than ever before, standardized assessments are being used to evaluate schools and teachers. Teachers are told each year that their students must exceed their current levels of performance, even if they are performing at or above grade level. This puts tremendous pressure on teachers and often causes conflict within them—should I spend classroom time teaching to the test or making sure my students have the knowledge they need in my subject area?

2. *Lack of time for planning, for preparation, and for taking care of personal needs:* Teachers' days are filled from the moment they walk in the door of the school until they leave the building, often with a satchel full of books and papers to grade. Even during their "planning" time, teachers often have to attend meetings, fill out forms, and meet with students—leaving very little time for preparing lessons, let alone for attending to personal needs such as going to the bathroom!

3. *Increasing performance requirements:* In addition to being experts in content areas, teachers are now expected to be computer literate, competent to counsel students on matters such as fam-

ily crises and drug abuse, effective public speakers, and skilled mediators.

4. *Dealing with challenging students:* It is not uncommon to find within one classroom students who may have different challenging needs. Some may have emotional and behavioral problems, various disabilities, or specific academic needs that challenge teachers in general education classrooms. In addition, there are more students than ever before for whom a language barrier exists.

5. *Dealing with a variety of parental needs:* Many parents of today's students do not speak English, so it is difficult for teachers to communicate with them verbally or in writing. Other parents may be difficult to communicate with because of their busy schedules or even apathy. Still others may hire advocates and attorneys to get what they want, thus cutting off direct parent–teacher communication. All these factors make it much more difficult for teachers to maintain an open dialogue with the parents of the students they teach.

6. *Individualizing instruction:* Students with disabilities, students who do not speak English, students who are tired, students who are gifted, students who are excused for sports events, and heterogeneous classes all contribute to the variety of academic and behavioral challenges that teachers must attend to on a daily basis. Coupled with insufficient planning and collegial time, it seems impossible to differentiate instruction to meet the wide variety of needs of the students found in today's classrooms.

7. *Lack of time for collegiality:* With students bringing such a variety of needs to the classroom, it is essential that teachers collaborate with their colleagues, such as grade- and subject-level teachers, psychologists, special education teachers, and curriculum specialists. Without the input of their colleagues, it is much more difficult for teachers to identify specific needs of the students and the most effective techniques to use with them.

8. *Lack of praise:* With increased pressure to excel in their subject area, find suitable ways to motivate and discipline their students, present material in interesting and creative ways, and ensure that their students do well on standardized tests, teachers need to

hear that they are doing a good job. Often, administrators are so busy assigning new tasks and evaluating their staff that they forget to acknowledge all the positive interventions teachers make on behalf of their students. They often fail to note the creativity teachers bring to the classroom on a daily basis and the work that they do to keep up with planning lessons, grading papers, contacting parents, and dealing with students' personal problems. Many teachers say that they have not heard anything positive from their supervisors in years!

Clearly, there are many things happening in the professional lives of teachers that may result in teacher distress. Many teachers succumb to these stressors, as indicated by the number of educators who leave the classroom because they feel burned out. Some teachers who leave the classroom go into administrative and support work; others leave the field completely. Research shows that if teachers or people in any other professions are to be happy in their jobs, they must get their motivational needs met (Bavendam, 2001; Perie & Baker, 1997; Pertz, 2000). More importantly, in order for teachers to have energy to individualize instruction and to shift to each student's frame of reference (i.e., to teach effectively), the teachers themselves must get their motivational needs met. Otherwise, they may burn out or look for another job that will provide greater job satisfaction.

Although it is each person's responsibility to get his or her own needs met, the best gift that teachers and principals can give their colleagues is to help them stay motivated. How can teachers and principals help? Most teachers have Workaholic, Persister, and Reactor as their most well-developed personality types. Workaholics and Persisters need recognition for their work. Therefore, praising them when they have done something well is a good beginning, for example, giving them recognition at a staff meeting. Reactor teachers need to be recognized for being nice people. Something as simple as spending a few minutes talking to them each day assures them that they are appreciated.

PHASE DISTRESS BEHAVIORS

In Chapter 1 we discussed the phenomenon of phase changes and noted that two thirds of the people in the United States experience one or more phase changes in their lifetimes. This includes teachers, many of whom have experienced at least one phase change. *The importance of phase is that it determines current motivation.* Therefore, when people experience a phase change, their motivation and distress behaviors change. When individuals are in normal distress, they show the distress behaviors associated with their personality

Table 11.1. Teacher first-, second-, and third-degree distress sequences

Reactor phase	
First°	Overadapts to students or colleagues
Second°	Makes mistakes; lacks assertiveness in class
Third°	Gets rejected: "I didn't feel liked."
Workaholic phase	
First°	Overthinks for students
Second°	Overcontrols, is critical of students around thinking issues
Third°	Rejects: "They can't even think."
Persister phase	
First°	Focuses on what students did wrong, instead of what they did right
Second°	Pushes beliefs; crusades and preaches in class
Third°	Forsakes students: "They don't have any commitment to learn."
Dreamer phase	
First°	Doesn't attend to students' needs
Second°	Passively waits; avoids students
Third°	Gets left out of activities: "Nobody told me what they wanted me to do."
Rebel phase	
First°	Tries hard to be on top of things but isn't
Second°	Blames things, situations, colleagues, or students
Third°	Gets vengeful: "I'll show them."
Promoter phase	
First°	Expects students to fend for themselves
Second°	Manipulates; creates negative drama in the classroom or in the school
Third°	Abandons students: "Can't take it, huh!"

From Kahler, T. (1982). *Personality pattern inventory validation studies.* Little Rock, AR: Kahler Communications, Inc., and Kahler, T. (1995). *The Process Teaching Seminar.* Little Rock, AR: Kahler Communications, Inc.; adapted by permission.

phase. If they are in severe distress, however, they show the distress behaviors of their base personality. Table 11.1 lists the distress behaviors of each personality type. The following stories illustrate this concept. It is important to remember that teachers in distress are still good people. It is the behaviors that they show when in distress that need to be changed. The key to reducing these behaviors is helping people in distress get their motivational needs met positively.

A REACTOR TEACHER

Paula represents a typical Reactor elementary school teacher. Often, Reactors go into elementary school teaching because they have many opportunities to demonstrate their warm, caring, and sensitive nature. It is important to Paula that the students, parents, and other teachers like her.

I've been teaching in elementary school for 8 years. I like children, and I show my students every day that I care for them. They know that I like them, and they like me. Moreover, they learn a lot in my class. I feel it is important that all children are comfortable in my class so they are at ease and able to learn more.

I get a lot of positive feedback about my teaching from the kids and their parents as well as my principal. Sometimes I feel overwhelmed in class, however. When that happens, I can feel my nerve endings and the adrenaline rushes going to my head. It is a real physiological feeling that gets triggered by many things. If I seem to be losing control of the children, I get flustered and tense. Sometimes I feel like I want to cry.

I want people to like me, so I don't like to ask people to do things they do not want to do. When I am required to do this, I become kind of wishy-washy. For example, last week I had to ask some of the other teachers to do something required by the school system. I knew they did not want to do it, so I kept apologizing to them as I was explaining the task. I empathized with them, but I don't feel that it helped the situation.

I don't like to correct people because I don't want to hurt their feelings. Once when I was working with a group of teachers, we made a chart of our ideas to present to the rest of the staff. I noticed our recorder spelled a word wrong. I did not point it out to her because I did not want to embarrass her. Later, after everyone had left, I corrected the chart myself.

Sometimes I get into distress when there is an overwhelming amount of paperwork or when I don't get enough sleep. For example, at the end of the year I sometimes feel overwhelmed trying to get everything together. Not only do we have report card grades and comments but also cumulative math and reading progress charts. In these situations I tend to become discouraged and lose things. Then I spend so much time looking for things that I don't have time to do what is needed.

The times when I am in the most distress in the classroom are when there is a personal problem at home. One time, my daughter got really sick, and I couldn't concentrate on anything. I wanted to be home with her, and I found it really hard to stay in the classroom. I felt the same way when my cat died.

The worst distress I ever felt was when I had an administrator who completely lacked leadership ability. I needed instructional leadership, and he did not provide it. Staff meetings were a waste of time. No feedback was given to teachers. The administrator would cancel meetings at the last minute. He would go into his office, close the door, and pull down the shade. It felt alienating and destroyed the morale of the entire staff. We could not rely on him, even to discuss scheduling. That was the worst 6 months of my teaching career. I was always in distress. I didn't feel empowered. My thinking got clouded. I had difficulty focusing, and I would lose track of what I was doing. The students knew I was in distress because whatever mood I was in was reflected in their behavior. If I was tense, they got tense. I made a conscious effort to be cheerful, but I was not always successful. There was tension in my

voice, my tone of voice changed, I became unclear, I lost things, and I didn't always have materials ready. Unfortunately, the children thought my anger was directed at them.

Discussion

When Reactors initially get into distress, they tend to overadapt to others—their students, their colleagues, their principals, or their spouses and children. They may have a hard time making decisions and may lose control of their classes. As their distress intensifies, they make silly mistakes on things they know how to do. They may lack assertiveness in class, they may not be able to find things, and they may not have their materials ready when they need them. When they become overwhelmed by distress, they may get depressed because they feel rejected by their students and peers and feel that no one likes them. These are warning signs that Reactor teachers are not getting their needs met positively.

Table 11.2. Reactor phase action plan

Needs: Recognition of person and sensory stimulation

You need to be recognized as a special and unique person. Personal relationships are important to you, both at home and in your professional life. You need to be around people who like you and care about you and with whom you show warmth and caring. You'll work best as part of a team in which you feel accepted, wanted, and noticed as an individual. Here are some ways to meet this need for personal attention, appreciation, and sensory stimulation:

Professionally

- Seek out and make good friends at work.
- Be cordial when possible and make eye contact with students, colleagues, and parents.
- Ask colleagues about their families—be authentic.
- Keep photographs of loved ones in your classroom or office where you can see them often.
- Arrange your classroom in an attractive manner.
- Greet your students with a smile as they come in.
- Team-teach a lesson with someone who appreciates your personality.
- Sponsor a club such as art, cooking, or a social club.
- Celebrate student accomplishments with parties and social recognition.
- Sing Happy Birthday to students on their birthdays.
- Keep flowers or plants around your classroom, if possible.
- Wear soft and comfortable, albeit appropriate, clothes and shoes whenever possible.
- Once per week initiate a conversation with a new acquaintance or colleague.

Personally

- Say "I love you" to your spouse and children frequently to let them know you care.
- Arrange for 15 minutes per day of "special time," in which you come first and no one interrupts you.
- Join a group or a team with people with whom you can connect.
- Arrange to have lunch or dinner with a good friend at least weekly.
- Play tapes of your favorite music.
- Telephone a special friend that you have lost touch with.
- Keep a birthday file and send greetings to friends.
- Make a special place at home where you can relax and feel comfortable.
- Take long hot baths.
- Get massages.
- Try out saunas, steam baths, and whirlpools.
- Have friends over for a special serving of home-cooked food.
- Keep a diary of how you feel about things. If you have someone special in your life, write as if you were actually talking to them.

From Kahler, T. (1982). *Personality pattern inventory validation studies.* Little Rock, AR: Kahler Communications, Inc., and Kahler, T. (1995). *The Process Teaching Seminar.* Little Rock, AR: Kahler Communications, Inc.; adapted by permission.

As we saw in Chapter 1, Reactors need recognition of person and sensory stimulation. They need to know that people like them because they are warm, caring, sensitive human beings. They also need an environment that pampers their senses (e.g., one with comfortable chairs, a cozy, nest-like environment, pleasant smells, soft music). Table 11.2 suggests several things Reactor teachers can do to get their needs met.

A PERSISTER TEACHER'S STORY

Frank is an exemplary middle school English teacher. Because he was so conscientious and dedicated, he was promoted and is now the head of the eighth-grade English department of his middle school. Frank represents a typical Persister middle school teacher.

I believe I am an excellent teacher, but the thought of being observed teaching increases my stress level. I put a lot of pressure on myself as a teacher so that my lessons will be perfect. They do not always turn out that way, of course. The idea of someone else watching me teach an imperfect lesson is stressful for me. Sometimes I get so distressed that I have physical symptoms. I get so uptight that I believe I might explode. When that happens, I sometimes tend to focus on what the students are doing wrong instead of complimenting them for what they are doing right.

I think about the students, teachers, and the department from the time I get up in the morning until I go to bed at night. What am I going to do today? How can I do it perfectly? What strategies can I use to help the students learn? How can I encourage the teachers in my department to do their best? I have high expectations for myself and for my colleagues.

Because I expect a lot of myself as a teacher and want all of my lessons to be perfect, I plan them very carefully. Once, I devised an individual spelling program for each student. It was very stressful to stay on top of it, but I wanted to have the perfect individualized spelling plan. When I do not have time to plan a lesson thoroughly I become very stressed, even though these are some of the best lessons I have taught.

I expect a lot of my students, too. I believe that students should work hard in class and learn as much as they can. When they do not work to their full potential I sometimes reprimand them harshly; preach at them; or make biting, sarcastic remarks. I believe teachers should not do this, so I do not allow this to happen very often.

Now that I am the department head, I expect the teachers in my department to demonstrate high-quality teaching and to have a program that benefits the students. Some of the teachers might say I push them a little hard, but I believe that the way we educators teach determines the success or failure of our students. So I believe it is essential that we plan our lessons carefully, teach professionally to the best of our ability, and maintain discipline and control in the classroom. Sometimes I criticize teachers who I believe are not doing their best for their students. I also get angry with parents who don't seem to be supporting their children adequately.

Last week I had a conflict between what I believe (my educational philosophy) and what I had to ask the teachers to do. I believe we should be encouraging children to think creatively and should be teaching them right from wrong. Our school district insists that we "teach to the tests" that the students are going to take so that we can raise achievement test scores. I believe achievement test scores are important, but they should not be the force that determines what we are going to teach. I was in distress about having to convey those requirements to the teachers. I got angry at the school system and became very critical of them for forcing me to do this. Now I am faced with a moral dilemma. Can I continue to ask teachers to do something I do not believe in? If I am forced to do so, can I continue to work in the school system? I have not yet answered either question.

Discussion

Frank is a Persister in distress. When Persister teachers initially get into distress, they focus on what their students, colleagues, parents, or the central office have done wrong and ignore the things they have done right. They may insert parenthetical expressions in their sentences and may preach, become dogmatic, and ridicule students. As their distress intensifies, they may crusade and preach to their students about such things as appropriate behaviors and the importance of the subject matter to their futures. They may attack or tease students for their lack of commitment or for giving incorrect answers. When they are overwhelmed by distress they may give up on their students because of their lack of commitment to learn.

Many Persister teachers become department heads, principals, central office managers, and even superintendents. In these positions they may forget to praise their colleagues and instead focus on what they believe is not going well. They may attack others for their lack of commitment and push their beliefs in order to get people to adopt programs or agenda items that they believe in. Ultimately, they may fire other employees or have them transferred to other offices or positions.

These behaviors indicate that Persister educators are not getting their motivational needs met positively. As we saw in Chapter 1, Per-

Table 11.3. Persister phase action plan

Need: Conviction and recognition of work

It is important for you to lead a life consistent with your beliefs, values, and opinions. Whenever possible you like to exercise your influence, affecting the growth and direction of others. You need to be around others who share your high standards of integrity, dependability, and trust. You could meet your needs in the following ways:

Professionally

- Each day, prioritize what you believe will be the best investment of your time and energy to ensure quality of effort.
- Reaffirm daily to yourself the value of your accomplishments even before you review your "to do" lists.
- Make agendas for your classes.
- Reward yourself for dedicated service.
- Earn and display one or more awards or pictures with people you respect for their accomplishments.
- Review the mission statement to make sure goals and objectives are consistent.
- Share your work with others, and enjoy their positive feedback on the quality of your labors.
- Join a civic group (e.g., Jaycees, Rotary, Civitan).
- Make suggestions to appropriate people regarding your ideas for the improvement of the school, curriculum, or methodology.
- Organize a school charitable contribution campaign or get involved in an existing one.
- Speak to local groups about educational issues.
- Involve yourself with projects to improve student achievement.
- Write an article about good educational practices.
- Sponsor a Chemathon, Science of the Mind, It's Academic, or similar team.
- Serve on the board of local or state teachers associations and participate in their activities.

Personally

- Share the personal importance of your successes and accomplishments with family and friends.
- Ask family and friends for admiration and respect.
- Create and display your favorite slogans, mottos, and creeds.
- Keep a journal of insights you believe are important.
- Get involved in a political campaign.
- Teach and model your values and beliefs to children.
- Contribute to a worthy cause with time or money.
- Involve yourself in community activities.
- Write a letter to the editor about some important issue.
- Become a leader of Boy Scouts, Girl Scouts, or a similar organization.

From Kahler, T. (1982). *Personality pattern inventory validation studies.* Little Rock, AR: Kahler Communications, Inc., and Kahler, T. (1995). *The Process Teaching Seminar.* Little Rock, AR: Kahler Communications, Inc.; adapted by permission.

sisters need recognition for their work and their convictions. They need to hear "Good job, well done, great idea." It is very important to them to be respected and to have their opinions listened to. They may be able to get these needs met in school by serving on various school committees, especially ethics or curriculum committees or those that determine school policies. Table 11.3 suggests several things Persister teachers can do to get their recognition for work and conviction needs met.

Phase and Distress Behaviors

So far in this book we have talked about people's current motivation being determined by the phase they are in. In Chapter 1 we described how a phase change can alter an individual's interests and life path. When people move into another phase, their distress behaviors also change. In normal distress they will show the behaviors associated with their phase distress sequence. In severe distress, however, they will once again show the distress sequence of their base personality type. This story illustrates both phase and base distress behaviors.

A WORKAHOLIC TEACHER IN A DREAMER PHASE

Michelle is a Workaholic in a Dreamer phase. In times of normal distress she may show her Dreamer phase behaviors, and in severe distress she may show her Workaholic distress tendencies. As a Workaholic, it is important for Michelle to be recognized for doing a good job and to adhere to a time structure. As someone in a Dreamer phase, she also needs some alone time each day. Sometimes, when these needs are not met, she gets into distress.

I enjoy teaching and have a reputation of being a very effective high school social studies teacher. I have a good academic background. I know my subject matter. And I find imaginative and inventive ways to teach the material so that the kids learn and have fun doing so. Although I usually enjoy teaching, I find that some days I have a hard time dealing with excessive noise and confusion. When that happens I keep going until I cannot take the noise any longer, then I shut down. For example, yesterday the noise in the classroom was too loud and I could not stand it any more. There were about 10 minutes left in the class, so I told the class that I was through teaching them that day. They could spend the rest of the period teaching themselves the material, and it was their responsibility to learn the information. I then went to my desk and started shuffling papers. I was not comfortable doing this and could not get any work done because I kept thinking I was not a good teacher to act this way. Nonetheless, I could not bring myself to teach any more for the rest of the class.

The same thing happened last week at play rehearsal. I play the accompaniment for the school musical. There was a break in the rehearsal. The kids were laughing, talking, joking, and clowning around, and several of the musicians were playing different tunes or striking chords on their guitars. I could handle that. Then the director asked one of the stage hands to vacuum the stage. The noise of the vacuum cleaner was the straw that broke the camel's back. I couldn't take the roar of the vacuum cleaner on top of everything else. I tried to shut out the noise but couldn't. Suddenly, I couldn't think, and I had to leave the stage to get away from the noise. I went outside to be alone for about 15 minutes. By the time they were ready to resume the rehearsal, I had pulled myself together and was able to accompany the musicians again.

Some days I react quite differently when I get into distress. Usually, this is when one of the students does something "dumb." For example, last month I was reviewing a lesson with one class in preparation for a test. I had given the class a paper to do for homework the night before and was going over the questions and answers with the class the next day. Halfway through the class I called on one student, who reminded me that he had been absent the day before and had not gotten the paper. He had been sitting there all this time not doing anything, when all he had to do was tell me he did not have a paper at the beginning of class and I would have given him one! I was still angry with him when I went to my office to get the paper for him. When I walked into my office my student assistant was talking with her boyfriend instead of doing the work she had been assigned. This intensified my anger and I took it out on her. I shouted at her for not doing what she was supposed to be doing, and in the process I embarrassed her in front of her boyfriend. When I went back to the class, I was upset that I had lost my temper, and this disrupted my train of thought for the rest of the period.

Discussion

In the beginning stages of distress, Dreamers tend to withdraw within themselves and therefore don't attend to student needs. As their distress intensifies, Dreamers may shut down and passively wait for someone or something outside of themselves to provide direction. When they are overwhelmed by distress, Dreamer teachers may get depressed and feel inadequate and helpless because no one told them what to do.

In the first two examples of Michelle's distress, when she sat at her desk ignoring the students and when she left the rehearsal to go outside, she was overwhelmed by the noise and confusion. She withdrew to get her Dreamer solitude need met so that she would have enough energy to continue working with students for the remainder of the day. These types of behaviors are warning signs that could let Michelle (and her colleagues) know that she must take action to get her motivational needs met. In Chapter 1 we saw that Dreamers need their own private time and their own private space. They need some alone time every day. See Table 11.4 for a list of possible things Dreamer teachers can do to get their solitude need met.

Although Michelle is in a Dreamer phase, her base personality type is Workaholic, and she sometimes shows her Workaholic distress behaviors as well. Workaholic teachers in the beginning stages of distress overthink for their students and become overly critical. They may use big words when simple words would suffice and they may overqualify by inserting parenthetical expressions in their sentences in an effort to be more precise. As their distress intensifies, they may overcontrol and may be critical of students around think-

Table 11.4. Dreamer phase action plan

Need: Solitude

You need alone time, where you can spend time by yourself, undisturbed by people, noises, or outside demands. When you meet your need for solitude you feel better, work more productively, and are able to reflect on your life and your goals. Here are some examples of how you can satisfy this need.

Professionally

- Three or four times each day find a way to be alone for about 1 minute. Don't allow any interruptions and don't think about what you have to do. Just relax and let your mind wander.
- Brown bag your lunch occasionally and eat by yourself. Enjoy your alone time.
- Give yourself a few minutes of alone time at the beginning and end of each workday.
- When correcting papers find a quiet corner where you can be alone while you correct them.
- Read a good book that is relevant to your field.
- Set aside time to read journals or magazine articles that are relevant to your field.
- Plan regular times each day when you can work alone and not be disturbed.

Personally

- Take a morning or evening walk alone.
- Work in the garden alone.
- Develop a solitary hobby like stamp collecting, coin collecting, or bird watching.
- Schedule some time when you can be alone to meditate.
- Read a book on a subject that interests you.
- Write poetry or paint or engage in an activity where you can give free rein to your imagination.
- Go to a movie alone.

From Kahler, T. (1982). *Personality pattern inventory validation studies.* Little Rock, AR: Kahler Communications, Inc., and Kahler, T. (1995). *The process teaching seminar.* Little Rock, AR: Kahler Communications, Inc.; adapted by permission.

ing issues, such as when Michelle thought her student had done something "dumb." When overwhelmed with distress, Workaholic teachers may get depressed and may reject students or their colleagues because they see them as hopeless and not able to think straight. These types of behaviors could let Michelle know she must take time to get her Workaholic needs met. As we saw in Chapter 1, Workaholics need recognition for their work and to make sure that

Table 11.5. Workaholic phase action plan

Needs: Recognition for work and time structure

You take pride in your ability to think and perform and you are willing to work hard to reach your goals. You prefer to set your own goals but can also work as a team player to accomplish something you accept as worthwhile. Achievement is important to you, and you need to recognize not only your own work but also to have others recognize your accomplishments. For example,

Professionally

- Set short-, medium-, and long-term goals, and check your progress regularly.
- Take time each day to set priorities and focus on doing what's most important.
- Recognize each day what you have accomplished before setting goals for the next day.
- Make lists and cross items off as you complete them.
- Develop a syllabus with assignments and due dates.
- Reward yourself for jobs accomplished.
- Earn and display one or more certificates, plaques, or awards for your accomplishments.
- Share your ideas with others.
- Work from "to do" lists.
- Purchase and use an organizer or plan book.
- Be careful not to take on more projects than you have time for.
- Be direct and honest about what you can and cannot do.
- Give yourself adequate time to be on time for school, meetings, and classes.
- Wear a watch and keep clocks in all important areas.

Personally

- Identify and firm up important personal rituals.
- Explain time structure needs to family or friends and ask for cooperation.
- Schedule some time that can be "cheerfully wasted" each day.
- Structure regular time to be spent with family or friends. Plan how you want to use this time.
- Plan a vacation.
- Set realistic times for going to bed and getting up to allow for rest and relaxation.
- Tell family members about your successes and accomplishments.
- Keep a journal.
- Use daily affirmations such as "I'm good enough without being perfect," and "I can and will meet my goals."
- Learn to play tennis, golf, racketball, or any sport where you can enjoy achieving.
- Paint, write, or engage in a hobby where you can see results immediately.

From Kahler, T. (1982). *Personality pattern inventory validation studies.* Little Rock, AR: Kahler Communications, Inc., and Kahler, T. (1995). *The process teaching seminar.* Little Rock, AR: Kahler Communications, Inc.; adapted by permission.

their time is structured. They need to hear "Good job," "Great idea," "Well done." They also need things to be organized, structured, and run on time. Table 11.5 provides further ideas for Workaholic teachers to get their needs met positively.

REBEL TEACHER IN A REACTOR PHASE

Anita is a special education teacher and coordinator in an elementary school. Her Reactor phase motivation is personal recognition, and in normal distress she will show Reactor phase behaviors. These were discussed in Paula's story. Her secondary motivation is to have fun. When she gets into severe distress, she may force other people to do things for her, may not give adequate instructions for people to do what she wants them to do, and may blame others when things go wrong.

I've been a special education teacher for 12 years, and now I also coordinate all of the special education programs in my building. I got into this field because I care deeply about children with disabilities and wanted to help them. My students like me, and I get along well with the other teachers. I am very creative, and I do a lot of fun things in class to help my students learn.

I rarely get into distress when I'm dealing with the kids. Sometimes I really get angry when I am dealing with other adults, though, including the teachers in my school, parents who attack me for not caring about their children, or central office staff who make bureaucratic decisions that I don't like. Initially, when I get ticked off I ask other people to do things for me. I may leave mundane things such as preparing reports or shuffling paper to others. Or I might not do them at all.

I also make sarcastic remarks. For example, when teachers make comments at staff meetings such as "You didn't remind me to do that," I might snap back with a sarcastic remark such as "Well, you didn't remind me to remind you." If a parent comes in and starts to verbally

attack me, my initial reaction is to feel hurt and get defensive. If they continue to attack, I may make some sarcastic remark that pushes the blame onto them. Last week a parent accused me of being a bureaucrat who is not interested in his child and who only cares about pushing paper and doing things to satisfy the bureaucracy. The two things I am most proud of are my concern for the children in my charge and the fact that I refuse to be a bureaucrat. I reacted by shouting back at him, telling him he didn't know what he was talking about, that he didn't know me if he thought those things about me, and that he'd better stop. Cooler heads interceded before the situation deteriorated any further.

I am most upset by bureaucratic decisions that superiors force on me. Last month, I worked out a program for a student with a developmental disability who was going to transfer to my school. The parents agreed this was the best program for the student. The teachers in the previous school agreed with the suggested program, and it was one that we could carry out with minimal cost. It would be a groundbreaking program for our school district, however. The principal and superintendent met with me and gave a list of reasons why it could not be done. The main reason was that it would set a precedent for our school district. They kept saying my decision affected the entire district and they would not authorize the program. I replied that this was the best program for this child and that it only affected this child in this school. They would not back down. I finally said, "If it weren't for you, we could provide this child with a superior program that meets her needs. I am going home." As I left I told my principal that I would not be in the next day. I was in so much distress that I could not think. I stayed home the next day and read all day long.

Once in a while, I get into distress in the classroom. This usually happens when I lose control of the class. Then I get angry and do some off-the-wall things to get the kids laughing. When they start laughing, I start laughing, too. Once that happens I am able to get myself out of distress and get them back under control. Every time I do something weird in the classroom I am afraid the children are going to tell their parents, but my principal has never said anything to me about it, so I guess they never do. They know my teaching methods are different, that I am human, and that I have their best interests at heart. Also, most of them like the way I teach.

Discussion

Anita is a Rebel in a Reactor phase. In the initial stages of distress she will show Reactor distress behaviors. Anita's first reactions when someone verbally attacks her are to feel hurt and get defensive. In severe distress she will show Rebel distress behaviors. In the initial stages of distress, Rebel teachers try hard to be on top of things, but really they are not. They tend not to give adequate instructions to enable students to do their assignments and do not delegate well. Also, they may cause other people to work harder by expecting them to do some of the less fun things, such as preparing papers or filling out forms. As their distress intensifies they blame things, situations, colleagues, or students when things go awry. They may say things such as "Yes, but . . . ." "If it weren't for you . . . ." or "See what you made me do." For example, Anita blamed her superintendent for not

Table 11.6. Rebel phase action plan

Need: Playful contact

You thrive on external stimulation. You dislike routine and simplicity so you need to be able to move around physically, move in and out of various situations and make contact with different people. You also need an environment with brightly colored lights, loud music, bright colors, and mechanical gadgets. You also like people who are fun and exciting to be around. You work best when you keep yourself charged up with lots of external stimulation. For example,

Professionally

- Decorate your classroom or office with lights, colors, gadgets, or wild posters.
- Play music periodically in class or between classes.
- Use your breaks and lunch hour to move around and visit with others.
- Take brief exercise and stretch breaks throughout the day.
- Attend professional conferences.
- Take a class or attend seminars or lectures with other educators in your field.
- Find creative ways to teach the subject matter, while staying in line.

Personally

- Go out dancing, go to a party, go to a large shopping mall, or go to an amusement park.
- Get some exercise or join a sports team.
- Join a community theater group and act in plays or musicals.
- Play a musical instrument and join a band or a choral group.
- Sketch cartoons or draw pictures.
- Design web pages or play computer games.

From Kahler, T. (1982). *Personality pattern inventory validation studies.* Little Rock, AR: Kahler Communications, Inc., and Kahler, T. (1995). *The Process Teaching Seminar.* Little Rock, AR: Kahler Communications, Inc.; adapted by permission.

providing the best program for her student. When overwhelmed by distress, Rebel teachers may get depressed and get censured because they ignore the rules, use offbeat teaching methods, and adopt an "I'll show you" attitude. If Anita were not such an outstanding teacher, her principal and superintendent might very well have censured her for her belligerent attitude and for leaving school and staying home.

These behaviors might let Anita know that she is not getting her Rebel needs met. As we saw in Chapter 1, Rebels need to have fun. They also need elements in an environment that turn them on (e.g., loud music, bright colors, posters, mechanical toys). Table 11.6

lists several things Rebel teachers might do to help them get their motivational needs met positively.

A PERSISTER TEACHER IN A PROMOTER PHASE

Donald teaches physical education in a vocational school. He is a Persister in a Promoter phase. In normal distress he will show his Promoter phase behaviors. In severe distress he will show his Persister base distress behaviors. We examined Persister distress behaviors in Felicia's story. This story will focus on Promoter distress behaviors.

I consider myself an excellent PE teacher. I know my stuff and can make my classes exciting, challenging, and action-oriented for my students. Most of the students enjoy my classes. I really know how to work with these kids who are in the vocational program. Many of them have short attention spans and like to work with their hands and bodies. I've created a rotating program that keeps the kids interested because they change activities frequently, keep their own scores, and challenge themselves to improve.

One of the teachers in the automotive program was having trouble with some of the same students who were responding very positively in my class. He wanted to know something about the system that I was using with them. I'm really proud of this method I've developed, so I started to tell him about it and to help him figure out how to set it up in his class. But then I heard that he told the principal about it and presented himself in a really positive light. I thought that maybe he hadn't told him that it was really my idea. I started to resent that he was using my techniques to make himself look good. So I just stopped showing up for our sessions where I had been showing him my stuff. I also didn't answer his e-mail. When he confronted me and said he still needed my support, I was short with him and said I didn't have the time to help him anymore. I know he felt abandoned by me, but I

wasn't going to let him use my own stuff to upstage me. Let him stand on his own two feet!

When I really want something and it doesn't look like I'm going to get it, I can promote myself very aggressively. I ignore protocol and bypass my superiors. Sometimes I've gone directly to the superintendent.

Unfortunately, now my superiors don't trust me. Some of them may even hate me. For example, last month I was trying to get one of my programs approved. My principal was not enthusiastic about the project, so I went to all of my peers trying to get their support. Some were opposed to the project, so I went to others and told them those who were opposed to the project were saying negative things about them. That's how I got several members of the staff to support me.

My principal still was not convinced, so I went to the central office building and spoke directly to the assistant superintendent. I am very persuasive, and she endorsed my project. When my principal found out what I had done, he was furious, but I don't care. I got what I wanted. Besides, I told the assistant superintendent some stories about my principal so that she wouldn't listen to my principal when he complains about me or my project. When my principal reprimanded me, I made up some stories that I said the superintendent had told me about him. When I get in distress, divide and conquer is my motto.

Table 11.7 Promoter phase action plan

Need: Incidence, excitement

You have a need for excitement and thrills so that you don't become bored, restless, or agitated. You also like challenges, risks, and competition—short-term goals with quick results or large payoffs. Be active in your life. Take charge of your need for incidence by setting up personal or professional challenges, engaging in new projects that are risky yet not too threatening to your well-being. Involve yourself with exciting, action-oriented people. Here are some suggestions of ways you can get your excitement need met:

Professionally

- Get involved in exciting projects.
- Find more active and exciting ways to present the subject matter.
- Brainstorm about better ways to do things.
- Take a chance on making long-shot suggestions to supervisors and colleagues.
- Seek out co-workers to have fun and exciting times with, so that work time is not dull or routine.
- Create action-oriented lessons.
- Consider changing directions. Look into getting into more action-oriented or exciting areas of teaching or administration.
- Get involved in projects that give quick recognition or rewards.

Personally

- Invest in higher risk stocks.
- Go to the horse races.
- Organize a costume party.
- Drive a go-kart or racing car.
- Join an aerobics or karate class.
- Get a pilot's license.
- Write adventure novels.

From Kahler, T. (1982). *Personality pattern inventory validation studies.* Little Rock, AR: Kahler Communications, Inc., and Kahler, T. (1995). *The Process Teaching Seminar.* Little Rock, AR: Kahler Communications, Inc.; adapted by permission.

Discussion

As mentioned previously, Donald is a Persister in a Promoter phase. We have already seen what Persisters in distress will do. This story illustrates what Promoter phase teachers might do in distress. As we saw in Chapter 1, Promoters need action and excitement. When they do not get these needs met positively they exhibit some predictable distress behaviors. In the initial stages of distress, Promoter phase teachers may not provide adequate support for their students or their colleagues. They expect them to be independent and fend for themselves. As their distress intensifies, Promoter teachers may manipulate and create negative drama in the classroom, with their peers, or among their superiors. Sometimes they do this by setting up negative drama such as Donald did among his peers and between his principal and superintendent. When they are overwhelmed by distress, Promoter phase teachers may abandon their students or their colleagues and leave them to fend for themselves.

As we saw in Chapter 1, Promoters need action and excitement. They may get these needs met positively by setting up action-oriented classes and providing exciting activities for their students. Table 11.7 suggests ways for Promoter phase teachers to get their needs met positively.

CONCLUSION

It is important that teachers get their motivational needs met every day or at least weekly. When Persister and Workaholic teachers are praised for their work and when Reactor teachers are recognized for their positive presence, they become more effective in their classrooms and have more energy to individualize their instruction. This increases the likelihood that each of their students will achieve to their fullest potential. Conversely, if teachers do not get their needs met regularly they will get into distress, fail to perform to their abilities, and may become dissatisfied with teaching as a profession. More important, they may lose their ability to reach and teach every student. When teachers do exhibit distress behaviors, it is important for everyone to remember that they are not purposely behaving this way but are responding to events that distress them. It is possible for these behaviors to change. Giving sincere compliments and recognition that are appropriate for each of the six personality types is a useful technique for helping teachers stay out of distress. When teachers get what they need, they can use their full potential to help every student succeed in school.

REFERENCES

Armstrong, T. (1994). *Multiple Intelligences in the classroom.* Alexandria, VA: Association for Supervision and Curriculum Development.

Bailey, R. (1998). *An investigation of personality type of adolescents who have been rated by classroom teachers to exhibit inattentive and/or hyperactive-impulsive behaviors.* Unpublished doctoral dissertation, University of Arkansas, Little Rock.

Bailey, R., & Gilbert, M. (1999, April). *An affirmation of suspicions: Identification of ADHD behaviors and classroom applications.* Paper presented at the annual convention of the Council for Exception Children, Charlotte, NC.

Bandler, R. (1988). *Learning strategies: Acquisition and conviction.* [videotape]. Boulder, CO: NLP Comprehensive.

Bavendam, J. (2001, May). *Managing job satisfaction* (On-line). Mercer Island, WA: Bavendam Research. (Available: http://www .employeesatisfactions.com)

Bradley, D.F., & Graves, D.K. (1997). Student support networks. In D.F. Bradley, M.E. King-Sears, & D.M. Tessier-Switlick, Teaching students in inclusive settings: From theory to practice (pp. 384–403.) Needham Heights, MA: Allyn & Bacon.

Bradley, D.F., Pauley, J.A., & Pauley, J.F. (2001). [Stresses in teaching]. Unpublished raw data.

Bradley, D.F., & Smith, K.D. (1999, September). The Process Communication Model: An effective tool to motivate all students. *Classroom Leadership Online, 3*(1), 1–5. (Available: http://www .ascd.org/pubs/cl/1sep99.html)

Dodd, A.W. (1995). Engaging students: What I learned along the way. *Educational Leadership, 53*(1), 65–67.

Gardner, H. (1983). *Frames of mind: The theory of Multiple Intelligences.* New York: Basic Books.

Gilbert, M. (1992, June). Dreamers, rebels, and others: Personality styles affect communication. *Executive Educator, 16*(6), 32–33.

Gilbert, M. (1994). *Meeting the needs of students can promote success.* Unpublished off-campus duty assignment report, University of Arkansas, Little Rock.

Gilbert, M. (1996, March). The Process Communication Model: Understanding ourselves and others. *NASSP Bulletin, 80*(578), 75–80.

Gilbert, M., & Bailey, R. (2000, January). *Understanding student preferences as a means of reducing their at-riskness.* Presentation at the Sixth Joint Annual Conference on Alternatives to Expulsion, Suspension, and Dropping Out of School, Orlando, FL.

Jackson, M.J., & Pauley, J.A. (December, 1999). Funsters and feelers: Students thrive with teaching that suits their natures. *Momentum, 30*(4), 37–40.

Jensen, E. (1995). *Super teaching.* San Diego: The Brain Store.

Kagan, S. (1994). *Cooperative learning.* San Juan Capistrano, CA: Kagan Cooperative Learning.

Kahler, T. (1974, January). The miniscript. *Transactional Analysis Journal, 4*(1). 22–42.

Kahler, T. (1979). *Process therapy in brief.* Little Rock, AR: Human Development Publications.

Kahler,T. (1982). *Personality pattern inventory validation studies.* Little Rock, AR: Kahler Communications, Inc.

Kahler, T. (1995). *The Process Teaching Seminar.* Little Rock, AR: Kahler Communications, Inc.

Kahler, T. (1995, January). A brief passing through. *Transactional Analysis Journal, 25*(1), 57–64.

Kahler, T. (1996). *Personality pattern inventory.* Little Rock, AR: Kahler Associates, Inc.

Kahler, T. (2000). *The mastery of management.* Little Rock, AR: Kahler Communications, Inc.

Loomans, D., & Kolberg, K. (1995). *The laughing classroom: Everyone's guide to teaching with humor and play.* Tiburon, CA: H.J. Kramer.

Perie, M., & Baker, D. (1997, August). *Statistical analysis report: Job satisfaction among America's teachers: Effects of workplace conditions, background characteristics, and teacher compensation* (On-line; NCES Publication No. 97-471). Washington, DC: National Center for Education Statistics. (Available: http://nces.ed.gov/pubsearch)

Pertz, P. (2000, August). *Labor Day survey uncovers myths about keeping great employees* (On-line). Pittsburgh: Development Dimensions International. (Available http://www.ddiworld.com)

Pool, C.R. (1997). Up with emotional health. *Educational Leadership, 54*(8), 12–14.

Rogers, S., & Renard, L. (1999). Relationship-driven teaching. *Educational Leadership, 57*(1), 34–37.

Rosen, M.D., & Weinstock, V.F. (1999). Class handout from Montgomery County Public Schools, MD.

Savage, R.V. (1991). *Discipline for self-control.* Upper Saddle River, NJ: Prentice Hall.

Smith, K.D., & Pauley, J.F. (1999, April). *What to do about Bernie: Teaching and reaching the hard-to-reach student.* Paper presented at the national conference of the Council for Exceptional Children, Charlotte, NC.

Stansbury, P. (1990). *Report of adherence to theory discovered when the personality pattern inventory was administered to subjects twice.* Little Rock, AR: Kahler Communications, Inc.

Wubbels, T., Levy, J., & Brekelmans, M. (1997). Paying attention to relationships. *Educational Leadership, 54*(7), 82–86.

APPENDIX

As you read through *Here's How to Reach Me: Matching Instruction to Personality Types in Your Classroom*, you may have formed an opinion of your base personality and phase. The surest way to determine that is to visit the authors' website (http:/www.kahlercom.com) and complete the personality structure questionnaire. If you would prefer a shortcut, however, this appendix will provide some suggested ways to help you decide your base and phase personality types.

One way to determine your base personality is to review the sets of adjectives listed in Chapter 1, Table 1.1, which lists the characteristics and perceptions of types. For example, are you compassionate, sensitive, and warm? If so, you have Reactor very well developed in your personality structure. Are you conscientious, dedicated, and observant? If so, you have Persister well developed. Are you responsible, logical, and organized? If so, then Workaholic is well developed. If you were to take the character strengths listed on Table 1.1, such as *compassionate, logical,* and *dedicated* and rank them according to how closely they describe you, with 1 being the most accurate, in what order would you rank them? In other words, are you more compassionate than dedicated or logical? Are you more logical than dedicated and compassionate? If you said you were more compassionate than logical and more logical than dedicated, then you may be a base Reactor with Workaholic as your next most well-developed part, with Persister third.

Having done this first step, as another way to determine your personality and phase types let's now look at how you express yourself in terms of the perceptions listed on Table 1.1 (emotions, thoughts, opinions, inaction, reactions, and actions). As explained in Chapter 1, people use certain words when they talk that reflect their perception of the world. (See the various versions of the Goldilocks story and Table 1.1, both in Chapter 1 and the Perceptions Worksheet, shown as Table A.1 in this appendix.) To ensure that you are tuned in to the perceptions you use, try taping yourself telling a story from memory and then listen to the tape while doing a fre-

Table A.1. Perceptions Worksheet

Perception	Personality type associated with perception	Words frequently used	Frequency tally	Rank
Emotions (Feelings)	Reactor (Feeler)	I feel, I'm comfortable with, I appreciate, I care, happy, sad, I love, close friends		
Thoughts (Data)	Workaholic (Thinker)	Who, what, when, where, data, facts, information, I think, Our options are, Does that mean, time frames, schedules		
Opinions (Beliefs)	Persister (Believer)	In my opinion, We should, I believe, respect, values, admire, commitment, trust, dedication		
Inactions (Reflections)	Dreamer (Imaginer)	Time to reflect, Hold back, Wait for more direction, Don't want to rock the boat, Own space, Easy pace		
Reactions (Likes/Dislikes)	Rebel (Funster)	Wow!, I like, I don't like, I hate, don't want, fun, Great!, Terrific, Tell it like it is		
Actions (Doing)	Promoter (Doer)	Bottom line, Make it happen, Give it your best shot, Go for it, Enough talk, Let's do it		

From Kahler, T. (1995). *The Process Teaching Seminar.* Little Rock, AR: Kahler Communications, Inc.; adapted by permission.

quency count of the perceptions you used (this activity can also be done with a written story). The Perceptions Worksheet can be useful in doing this. What perception did you use the most? Emotions? Thoughts? What perception came in second and third in terms of frequency of use? Do these perceptions align with your ranking of the adjectives, in terms of personality type? If your base personality came out the same on the adjectives and on the perceptions you used, you can be fairly certain that that is your base personality type. How did you do on your personality structure? Do you know your base personality type now?

To give you an example of how to take a frequency count of the perceptions used in a speech, let's look at the first part of Lincoln's Gettysburg Address (see Figure A.1). In Figure A.2, the perceptions are marked to enable you to see how often Abraham Lincoln used a perception during this speech. As you will note, nearly every word is marked.

Next, see how the perceptions are tallied using the Perceptions Worksheet. As you will see, Lincoln used thoughts 35 times, opinions 13 times, actions 9 times, and emotions 2 times. This indicates that Lincoln was a Workaholic with Persister second, Promoter third, and Reactor fourth (see Table A.2).

Now for your phase. There are 36 possible combinations of base and phase. What is yours at this time? The best indicators of phase are how a person is motivated and what he or she does while in distress. Table 1.2 in Chapter 1 shows the motivation or need for each of the six personality types. How are you motivated? Do you want people to like you? Would you rather be respected than liked? Do you want people to tell you when you have done a good job? Do you need people to be on time for meetings? Look at your current motivation and see how that correlates with the structure of your condominium.

Now let's look at what you do in distress. Table 11.1 in Chapter 11 lists the distress behaviors and sequences that all six types of teachers show when in three degrees of distress. What do you do when you are in distress? What personality type does those things? What do you do to get yourself out of distress? Look at the suggested activities in the action plans for the personality types, given in Tables 11.2 through 11.7 at the end of Chapter 11. Which action plan do you think would help you the most? If you have a good match, that probably is the phase you are in.

Fourscore and seven years ago, our fathers brought forth on this continent, a new nation, conceived in liberty, and dedicated to the proposition that all men are created equal.

Now we are engaged in a great Civil War, testing whether that nation, or any nation so conceived and so dedicated, can long endure.

We are met on a great battlefield of that war. We have come to dedicate a portion of that field as a final resting place for those who here gave their lives that a nation might live. It is altogether fitting and proper that we should do this. But in a larger sense, we cannot dedicate—we cannot consecrate—we cannot hallow this ground. The brave men, living and dead, who struggled here, have consecrated it far above our poor power to add or detract. The world will little note nor long remember what we say here, but it can never forget what they did here.

It is for us the living, rather, to be dedicated here to the unfinished work which they who fought here have thus far so nobly advanced. It is rather for us to be here dedicated to the great task remaining before us—that from these honored dead we take increased devotion to that cause for which they gave the last full measure of devotion. That we here highly resolve that these dead shall not have died in vain: That this nation, under God shall have a new birth of freedom; and that government of the people, by the people, for the people, shall not perish from the earth.

—Abraham Lincoln, Gettysburg, November 19, 1863

Figure A.1. The opening remarks of Lincoln's Gettysburg Address.

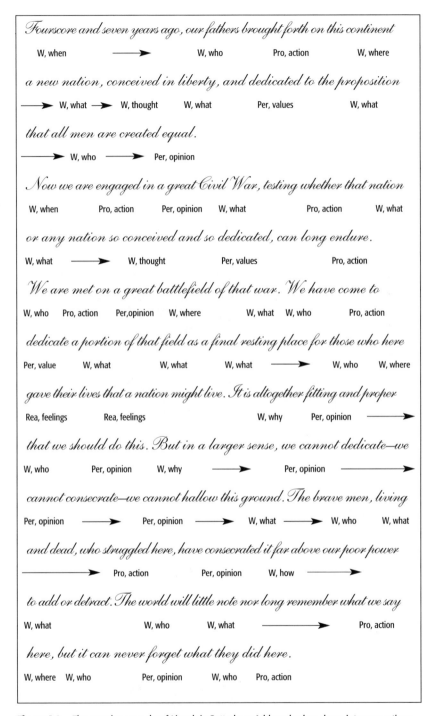

Figure A.2. The opening remarks of Lincoln's Gettysburg Address broken down into perceptions.

Table A.2. Perceptions Worksheet for Abraham Lincoln based on the opening of his Gettysburg Address

Perception	Personality type associated with perception	Words frequently used	Frequency tally	Rank
Emotions (Feelings)	Reactor (Feeler)	I feel, I'm comfortable with, I appreciate, I care, happy, sad, I love, close friends	2	4
Thoughts (Data)	Workaholic (Thinker)	Who, what, when, where, data, facts, information, I think, Our options are , Does that mean, time frames, schedules	35	1
Opinions (Beliefs)	Persister (Believer)	In my opinion, We should, I believe, respect, values, admire, commitment, trust, dedication	13	2
Inactions (Reflections)	Dreamer (Imaginer)	Time to reflect, Hold back, Wait for more direction, Don't want to rock the boat, Own space, Easy pace	0	5/6
Reactions (Likes/Dislikes)	Rebel (Funster)	Wow!, I like, I don't like, I hate, don't want, fun, Great!, Terrific, Tell it like it is	0	5/6
Actions (Doing)	Promoter (Doer)	Bottom line, Make it happen, Give it your best shot, Go for it, Enough talk, . Let's do it	9	3

From Kahler, T. (1995). *The Process Teaching Seminar.* Little Rock, AR: Kahler Communications, Inc.; adapted by permission.

You can use this same method to determine the base and phase of your students. If you are having a problem with some of your students, it is very possible that their base and phase are of the personality types that are least well developed in your personality structure. Therefore, review the character strengths and perceptions used by the personality types that are least well developed in your personality structure. Do the troublesome students have these strengths? Do they use these perceptions? Next, look at the student distress behaviors in Tables 9.1–9.6 in Chapter 9. Are the behaviors that are bothering you the ones that are listed as characteristic of the personality types that are least well developed in your personality structure? How can you motivate these students? Suggestions for reaching each of the personality types is given in these tables as well as in the tables in Chapters 2–7.

INDEX

Page numbers followed by *f* indicate figures; those followed by *t* indicate tables.

ABC charts, *see* Antecedent, behavior, consequence charts
Abstract mode learning style, 106
Accountability, as teacher stressor, 170
Action plans for teachers in distress
  Dreamer phase, 185*t*
  Persister phase, 181*t*
  Promoter phase, 193*t*
  Reactor phase, 177*t*
  Rebel phase, 190*t*
  Workaholic phase, 186*t*
Actions, perception through, 5, 16, 18
Active learning style, 106
Activities, classroom, *see* Classroom activities
Adaptability, as Promoter characteristic, 3*t*
ADHD, *see* Attention-deficit/hyperactivity disorder
Administrators
  adaptation of lesson planning questions, 151–152
  Persister teachers as, 180, 182
Affective learning area of the brain, 108
Aggression, Student Intervention Plan (SIP) for, 156*f*
Antecedent, behavior, consequence (ABC) charts, 160*f*, 161*f*, 163*f*
Appreciation, need for, as Reactor characteristic, 3, 24, 38–40, 39*t*
Assessing Matrix for Educators, 107*f*
Assessment, as teacher stressor, 170
Attention-deficit/hyperactivity disorder (ADHD)
  hyperactive impulsive type

    Dreamers and, 69
    Rebels and, 81
    Promoters and, 94
  inattentive type
    Dreamers and, 69
    Rebels and, 81,
    Promoters and, 94
  students in distress referred with, 29
Auditory mode learning style, 104–105, 107*f*

Behavior assessment, *see* Functional behavioral assessments (FBAs)
Behaviors, negative, *see* Distress
Bodily-kinesthetic intelligence, 103, 104*t*
Brain-based learning, 108–109, 109*t*

Channels of communication, 26*t*, 27–29
Charm, as Promoter characteristic, 3*t*, 5
Classroom activities
  "battery charge" introductions, 149–151
  Dreamers, 71*t*, 104*t*, 130*t*, 131, 157*f*
  emotional disabilities, students with, 148–149, 156*f*, 159
  group activities, 106, 107*f*, 148–149
  high school chemistry, 146, 148
  high school English, 149
  learning disabilities, for students with, 157*f*
  math, 143–144, 145*f*
  middle school science, 150

Classroom activities—*continued*
  Persisters, 59*t*, 104*t*, 127*t*, 128
  persuasive writing lesson, elementary school, 150
  Promoters, 96*t*, 104*t*, 137, 138*t*, 139
  Reactors, 39*t*, 104*t*, 120, 121*t*
  Rebels, 83*t*, 104*t*, 133, 134*t*, 135, 156*f*, 158*f*
  special education classes, 145–146, 147*f*, 149
  Workaholics, 48*t*, 104*t*, 123, 124*t*
  working alone, 106, 107*f*
Cognitive learning area of the brain, 108
Commitment, as Persister characteristic, 25, 25*t*
Communication
  channels of communication, 26*t*, 27–29
  see also Language of personality; Miscommunication
Compassion, as Reactor characteristic, 3, 3*t*, 38
Concrete mode learning style, 106
Conscientiousness, as Persister characteristic, 3*t*, 58–59
Cooperative learning, 109–112
Creativity
  Rebels, 3*t*, 5, 78, 82

Dedication, as Persister characteristic, 3*t*, 4–5, 58–59
Developmental disabilities, Workaholic students, 47
Direction, need for
  Dreamers, 5, 25, 28, 70, 71*t*
  Promoters, 28
Directive channel of communication
  described, 26*t*, 28
  with Dreamers, 74, 130, 130*t*
  with Promoters, 98–99, 137, 138*t*
Disabilities, students with
  developmental disabilities, 47
  emotional disabilities, 148–149
  learning disabilities, 26, 47
  see also Special education
Distress
  degrees of, 29–31, 30*f*, 117–118

  impact on students, 29–31, 116–118
  impact on teachers, 29–31, 172, 194–195
  reducing by meeting motivational needs, 23
  student reactions
    Dreamers, 26, 69–70, 128–129, 130*t*
    Persisters, 125–126, 127*t*
    Promoters, 26, 94, 98, 135–136, 138*t*
    Reactors, 119–120, 121*t*
    Rebels, 26, 82, 131–132, 134*t*
    Workaholics, 120–123, 124*t*
  teacher reactions
    Persister teacher in a Promoter phase, 173*t*, 191–194
    Persisters, 173*t*, 178–180, 182
    phase distress, 172–174, 173*t*
    Reactors, 173*t*, 174–176, 178
    Rebel teacher in a Reactor phase, 173*t*, 187–191
    Workaholic teacher in a Dreamer phase, 173*t*, 182–185, 187
Dreamer personality type
  attention-deficit/hyperactivity disorder (ADHD), 69
  characteristics of, 3*t*, 5, 69–71
  distress
    difficulties in school, 26, 29
    prevention/intervention methods, 129–131, 130*t*
    signs of distress, 128–129, 130*t*
    teacher behaviors, 173*t*
  interactions with teachers, 25, 64–69, 70–74
  learning strategies
    brain-based learning, 109*t*
    cooperative learning, 110, 112
    learning styles, 105–106, 107*f*
    multiple intelligences, 104*t*
    peer teaching, 113
  miscommunication example, 72–74
  motivational needs, 25, 25*t*, 71*t*
  percentage of, in population, 4*f*, 69
  phase changes, 173*t*
  praising, sample feedback, 166*f*

sample Student Intervention
Plans (SIPs) and intervention
strategy logs, 157*f*
storytelling example, 21
student example, 64–69
suggestions for supporting
students, 71*t*
teachers
action plan, 177*t*
distress behaviors, 173*t*
Workaholic teacher in a
Dreamer phase, 182–185, 187
written cues, 23
Dropouts, high incidence of in personality types, 29

Educational tools, *see* Instruction
methods
Einstein, Albert, as Dreamer, 70–71
Elementary school
persuasive writing lesson, 150
Reactors as teachers, 3, 10*f*,
174–176, 178
special education lesson planning, 145–146, 147*f*
Workaholics as teachers, 10*f*
Emotional disabilities, students
with, 148–149
Emotional well-being, importance
of for learning, 116
Emotions, perception through, 3,
3*t*, 15, 17
Emotive channel of communication
described, 26*t*, 29, 133, 134*t*
with Rebel, 133, 134*t*
Empathy, as Reactor characteristic,
3, 24, 40
Excitement, need for, as Promoter
characteristic, 25*t*, 26, 95, 96*t*
External/extrinsic motivation for
learning, 106, 107*f*

FBAs, *see* Functional behavioral
assessments
Feedback
importance of, 165
100+ PCM ways to praise a child,
166*f*

used in appropriate interventions,
167
Forms, sample
Functional Behavioral Assess-
ment (FBA) form, 160*f*
Intervention Strategy Log, 154*f*
Student Intervention Plan (SIP),
154*f*
Friendships
Dreamers, 64–65, 68, 72
Persisters, 55, 58
Promoters, 88, 92–93, 95
Reactors, 34–36, 38, 40
Rebels, 77, 78–79, 80–81
Workaholics, 46–47
Fun, need for, as Rebel characteris-
tic, 3*t*, 5, 25–26, 25*t*, 78, 80,
82, 83*t*, 86
Functional behavioral assessments
(FBAs)
antecedent, behavior, consequence
(ABC) charts, 161*t*, 163*t*
described, 142, 159–163, 165
evaluating reasons behind
behavior, 162*t*
motivations and interventions,
164*t*
sample assessment form, 160*f*

Gender ratios of personality types,
38, 47, 57, 69, 81, 94
Goals and objectives, in Student
Intervention Plans (SIPs), 159
Group activities, *see* Classroom
activities

High school
chemistry lesson planning, 146,
148
Persisters as teachers, 5, 7*f*
special education English lesson,
149
Workaholics as teachers, 4, 7*f*

Individualized education programs
(IEPs), use of in Student
Intervention Plans (SIPs), 159

Imagination, as Dreamer character-
    istic, 3t, 4, 5, 70–71
Inaction, see Reflection
Individualizing instruction, as
    teacher stressor, 171, 173t,
    182–185, 187
Information orientation, as Work-
    aholic characteristic, 4, 49
Instruction methods
    brain-based learning, 108–109, 109t
    cooperative learning, 109–112
    functional behavioral assess-
        ments (FBAs), 159–163, 160f,
        161t, 162t, 163t, 164t, 165
    learning styles, 104–106, 107f
    lesson planning questions,
        143–152, 144f, 145f, 147f
    multiple intelligences, 102–104,
        104t
    100+ PCM ways to praise a child,
        165, 166f, 167
    peer teaching, 112–115
    Student Intervention Plans (SIPs),
        153, 154f–158f, 159
Internal motivation for learning,
    106, 107f
Interpersonal intelligence, 103,
    104t
Intervention plans, see Student
    Intervention Plans (SIPs)
Intervention Strategy Log, see
    Forms, sample
Intrapersonal intelligence, 103,
    104t
Intrinsic motivation for learning,
    106, 107f

Kinesthetic intelligence, 103, 104t
Kinesthetic mode learning style,
    104–105, 107f

Language of personality
    channels of communication, 26t,
        27–29
    overview, 6, 8
    storytelling examples, 19–23
    verbal cues, 17–18
    written cues, 23

Learning
    classroom activities, in multiple
        intelligences method, 104t
    learning activities, brain-based
        learning, 109t
    learning styles, 104–106, 107f
    see also Instruction methods
Learning disabilities, students with
    Dreamers, 26, 157f, 159
    Promoters, 26
    Rebels, 26
    Workaholics, 47
Lesson planning questions, 142,
    143–152, 144f, 145f, 147f
Likes and dislikes, see Reactions,
    perception through
Linguistic intelligence, 103, 104t
Logic, as Workaholic characteristic,
    3t, 4, 25
Logical/mathematical intelligence,
    103, 104t
Loyalty, as Persister characteristic,
    4–5, 57–58

Math lesson planning questions,
    143–144, 145f
Mathematical intelligence, 103, 104t
Michelangelo, as Dreamer, 71
Middle school
    Persisters as teachers, 5, 7f,
        178–180, 182
    science lesson, 150
    Workaholics as teachers, 4, 7f
Miscommunication
    degrees of, 30–31, 30f
    Dreamers, 72–74
    examples, 26t
    Persisters, 60–61
    Promoters, 97–99
    Reactors, 40–41
    Rebels, 84–86
    Workaholics, 49–51
Mismatch of students and teachers,
    examples of, 6, 8
    see also Miscommunication
Motivational needs
    Dreamers, 25, 25t, 164t
    importance of addressing,
        167–168

overview, 23–27, 25t
Persisters, 25, 25t, 164t
Promoters, 25t, 26, 164t
Reactors, 24–25, 25t, 164t
Rebels, 25–26, 25t, 164t
teachers, 171–172
Workaholics, 25, 25t, 164t
Multiple intelligences, 102–104, 104t
Musical intelligence, 103, 104t

Naturalistic intelligence, 103, 104t
Needs of students, see Motivational
    needs
Negative behaviors, see Distress
Nurturative channel of communi-
    cation
    described, 26t, 28
    miscommunication with Work-
        aholics, 50–51
    with Reactors, 120, 121t
Nurturing, as Reactor characteris-
    tic, 3, 38–39, 40

100+ PCM ways to praise a child,
    165, 166f, 167
Opinions, perception through, 3t,
    4–5, 15, 17–18
Organization
    of social events, as Reactor char-
        acteristic, 40
    Workaholics' need for, 4, 25, 47,
        48

Parental needs, as teacher stressor,
    171
PCM, see Process Communication
    Model
Peer teaching, 112–115
Perception patterns, 3–5, 3t, 15,
    16–18
Performance requirements, as
    teacher stressor, 170–171
Persister personality type
    characteristics of, 3t, 4–5, 57–60
    distress
        prevention/intervention meth-
            ods, 126, 127t, 128

signs of distress, 125–126, 127t
    teacher behaviors, 173t,
        178–180, 181t, 182
    interactions with teachers, 25,
        55–56, 105
    learning strategies
        brain-based learning, 109t
        cooperative learning, 110, 112
        learning styles, 105, 106, 107f
        multiple intelligences, 104t
        peer teaching, 113
    miscommunication example,
        60–61
    motivational needs, 25, 25t, 59t
    percentage of, in population, 4f,
        57
    phase changes, 11–15, 173t,
        178–180, 181t, 182
    praising, sample feedback, 166f
    storytelling example, 20–21
    student example, 54–57
    suggestions for supporting
        students, 59t
    teachers
        action plan, 177t
        distress behaviors, 173t,
            178–180, 181t, 182
        interaction with Reactor stu-
            dent, 40–42
        interaction with Rebel student,
            84–86
        phase changes, 11–15, 16f
        profile, 5, 6, 7f, 8
    written cues, 23
Personality types
    channels of communication, 26t,
        27–29
    characteristics of, 3–5, 3t
    development, 6
    languages of, 6, 8
    motivational needs, 23–27
    percentage of, in population, 4f
    perceptions, 3–5, 3t, 15, 16–18
    phases, 11–15, 16f
    see also Dreamer; Persister; Pro-
        moter; Reactor; Rebel;
        Workaholic
Phase changes
    influence on motivation, 11
    Persister teacher, 11–15, 16f

Phase changes—*continued*
  phase distress behaviors,
      172–174, 173*t*
Praise, *see* Feedback
Principals
  Persister teachers as, 180, 182
Process Communication Model
    (PCM)
  incorporating with multiple
      intelligences theory, 102,
      104*t*
  overview, 2
Promoter personality type
  attention-deficit/hyperactivity
      disorder (ADHD), 94
  characteristics of, 3*t*, 5, 94–97
  distress
    difficulties in school, 26, 29, 94
    prevention/intervention meth-
        ods, 136–137, 138*t*, 139
    signs of distress, 135–136, 138*t*
    teacher behaviors, 173*t*
  interactions with teachers, 89–90,
      94, 95–99
  learning strategies
    brain-based learning, 109*t*
    cooperative learning, 111, 112
    learning styles, 105, 106, 107*f*
    multiple intelligences, 104*t*
    peer teaching, 114
  miscommunication example,
      97–99
  motivational needs, 25*t*, 26, 96*t*
  percentage of, in population, 4*f*, 94
  phase changes, 173*t*
  praising, sample feedback, 166*f*
  storytelling example, 22–23
  student example, 88–94
  suggestions for supporting stu-
      dents, 96*t*
  teachers
    action plan, 177*t*
    distress behaviors, 173*t*
    Persister teacher in a Promoter
        phase, 173*t*, 191–194
  written cues, 23
Psychological needs, *see* Motiva-
    tional needs
Psychomotor learning area of the
    brain, 108

Reactions, perception through, 5,
    15, 18
Reactor personality type
  characteristics of, 3, 3*t*, 38–40
  distress
    prevention/intervention meth-
        ods, 119–120, 121*t*
    signs of distress, 118–119, 121*t*
    teacher behaviors, 173*t*,
        174–176, 178
  interactions with teachers, 24–25,
      36–37, 38–42
  learning strategies
    brain-based learning, 109*t*
    cooperative learning, 110, 112
    learning styles, 105, 106, 107*f*
    multiple intelligences, 104*t*
    peer teaching, 112–113
  miscommunication example,
      40–41
  motivational needs, 24–25, 25*t*,
      39*t*
  percentage of, in population, 4*f*,
      38
  phase changes, 14–15, 173*t*,
      174–176, 177*t*, 178
  praising, using feedback while,
      166*f*
  sample Student Intervention Plan
      (SIP) and Intervention Strat-
      egy Log, 155*f*
  storytelling example, 19
  student example, 34–38
  suggestions for supporting stu-
      dents, 39*t*
  teachers
    action plan, 177*t*
    distress behaviors, 173*t*,
        174–176, 178
    interaction with Dreamer stu-
        dent, 70
    interaction with Workaholic
        student, 49–51
    profile, 3, 8, 10*f*
  written cues, 23
Rebel personality type
  attention-deficit/hyperactivity
      disorder (ADHD), 81
  characteristics of, 3*t*, 5, 9*f*, 81–82
  distress

difficulties in school, 8, 26, 29, 82, 86
prevention/intervention methods, 132–133, 134t, 135
signs of distress, 131–132, 134t
teacher behaviors, 173t
interactions with teachers, 8, 77, 79, 81–86
learning strategies
brain-based learning, 109t
cooperative learning, 111, 112
learning styles, 105, 106, 107f
multiple intelligences, 104t
peer teaching, 113–114
miscommunication example, 84–86
motivational needs, 25–26, 25t, 83t
percentage of, in population, 4f, 81
phase changes, 13–15, 173t
praising, sample feedback, 166f
sample Student Intervention Plans (SIPs) and intervention strategy logs, 156f, 158f
storytelling example, 21–22
student example, 76–81
suggestions for supporting students, 83t
teachers, 13–14, 16f, 72–74
action plan, 177t
distress behaviors, 173t
interaction with Dreamer student, 72–74
Rebel phase, 13–14, 16f
written cues, 23
Recognition, need for
Persisters, 25, 25t, 58–59, 61
Reactors, 24–25, 25t, 40
teachers, 171–172
Workaholics, 25, 25t, 47–48, 51
Reflection, perception through, 5, 15, 18
Reflective learning style, 106
Requestive channel of communication
described, 26t, 28, 123, 124t, 126, 127t
with Persister, 126, 127t
with Workaholic, 123, 124t

Resourcefulness, as Promoter characteristic, 3t, 5
Responsibility
Persisters, 58–60
Workaholics, 3t, 4, 49
Routine
Persisters' ability to follow, 57, 60
Promoters' dislike of, 93, 95
Rebels' dislike of, 76, 82
Workaholics' need for, 25, 25t, 48
Rules, ability to follow, as Persister characteristic, 56, 58

School, difficulty in
Dreamers, 26, 29
Promoters, 26, 29
Rebels, 26, 29
see also Distress
Sensitivity, as Reactor characteristic, 3, 3t, 38
Sensory stimulation, need for, as Reactor characteristic, 24, 25t, 38
Solitude, need for, as Dreamer characteristic, 25, 25t, 66–67, 74
Spatial intelligence, 103, 104t
Special education
high school English lesson, 149
lesson planning, elementary school, 145–146, 147f
Reactors as teachers, 3
students in distress referred for, 29
Spontaneity, as Rebel characteristic, 3t, 5
Stress
reactions to, 116–118
teacher stressors, 170–172
see also Distress
Student Intervention Plans (SIPs), 142, 153, 154f–158f, 159
Student needs, see Motivational needs

Tactile/kinesthetic mode learning style, 104–105, 107f

Tattling, as Persister characteristic, 60

Teachers
  action plans, professional and personal
    Dreamer phase, 185t
    Persister phase, 181t
    Promoter phase, 193t
    Reactor phase, 177t
    Rebel phase, 190t
    Workaholic phase, 186t
  distress
    Persister teacher in a Promoter phase, 173t, 191–194
    Persisters, 173t, 178–180, 182
    Reactors, 173t, 174–176, 178
    Rebel teacher in a Reactor phase, 173t, 187–191
    Workaholic teacher in a Dreamer phase, 182–185, 187
  Persisters, 5, 6, 7f, 8, 16f, 40–42, 84–86
  Reactors, 3, 8, 10f, 49–51, 70
  Rebels, 13–14, 16f, 72–74
  Workaholics, 4, 6, 7f, 8, 10f, 16f, 60–61, 97–99

Thoreau, Henry David, as Dreamer, 71

Thoughts, perception through, 3t, 4, 15, 17

Thrill-seeking, as Promoter characteristic, 26, 95

Time constraints, as teacher stressor, 170, 171

Time structure, need for, as Workaholic characteristic, 25, 25t, 48

Values, importance of, as Persister characteristic, 5, 25, 57–59

Verbal cues for patterns of perception, 17–18

Visual mode learning style, 104–105, 107f

Warmth, as Reactor characteristic, 3t

Warning signs of distress, see Distress

Work ethic
  Persisters, 60
  Workaholics, 25

Workaholic personality type
  characteristics of, 3t, 4, 47–49
  distress
    prevention/intervention methods, 123, 124t
    signs of distress, 120–123, 124t
    teacher behaviors, 173t, 182–185, 187
  interactions with teachers, 25, 44–45, 47
  learning strategies
    brain-based learning, 109t
    cooperative learning, 110, 112
    learning styles, 105, 106, 107f
    multiple intelligences, 104t
    peer teaching, 113
  miscommunication example, 49–51
  motivational needs, 25, 25t, 48t
  percentage of, in population, 4f, 47
  phase changes, 12–13, 173t
  praising, sample feedback, 166f
  storytelling example, 19–20
  student example, 44–47
  suggestions for supporting students, 48t
  teachers
    action plan, 177t
    distress behaviors, 173t, 182–185, 187
    interaction with Promoter student, 97–99
    phase changes, 12, 16f
    profile, 4, 6, 7f, 8, 10f
    written cues, 23
  Written cues, language of personality, 23